JACQUELINE GELLENS WATSON

THE

Habit

Book design by Epic Author Publishing

Contact: 800-273-1625 | support@epicauthor.com | EpicAuthor.com

TO MY sister, Wilma, who helped me so much when I was growing up, especially with her sense of humor.

To Mother and Daddy, who gave me high standards to pursue.

To my seven step-children, who helped me through my periods of grief and for their devotion.

To my doctors, all of them.

ABOUT THE BOOK

THE HABIT is about Obsessive-Compulsive Disorder suffered by a small-town girl leading her to make many mistakes in life.

It's not written as a tragedy but hopefully will help others to face the consequences of their disorder and find help and continue with it until they have the illness, which it is, under control.

"I think the mistakes we make are the price we pay for having an interesting life." –Jackie Watson

This not an excuse, but it does bring me some solace.

I hope you enjoy the book.

Jackie

JACQUELINE GELLENS WATSON
Wilmington, DE

ACKNOWLEDGMENTS

FIRST, I'd like thank you, the reader for picking up this book.

I hope you find it valuable.

Second, I'd like to thank a few of the people who helped make this book possible.

Special thanks to Ernie Purnell Sr. and Mark Purnell, who helped me contact Trevor Crane, my publisher, and Hilary Jastram, my editor.

To Viga B. Hall Jr., my life-long friend, who wrote my foreword.

To Kathi Lewis for your original editing.

To Nancy Pinson, Beverly Guinto and Dick Fox for your computer expertise and invaluable guidance and assistance.

To Joan Kovach for her beautiful painting that adorns the front of this book.

Finally, I wrote this book to help people.

I hope it helps you, or someone you care about.

CONTENTS

FOREWORD   vii

INTRODUCTION   xi

SECTION ONE: **THE BREAK**   1

     CHAPTER 1   3

SECTION TWO: **UNDIAGNOSED**   7

CHAPTER 2 9	CHAPTER 25 105	CHAPTER 48 . . . 203
CHAPTER 3 15	CHAPTER 26 109	CHAPTER 49 . . . 205
CHAPTER 4 17	CHAPTER 27 113	CHAPTER 50 . . . 209
CHAPTER 5 21	CHAPTER 28 117	CHAPTER 51. 211
CHAPTER 6 27	CHAPTER 29 119	CHAPTER 52 213
CHAPTER 7 31	CHAPTER 30 123	CHAPTER 53 217
CHAPTER 8 37	CHAPTER 31 129	CHAPTER 54 223
CHAPTER 9 41	CHAPTER 32 133	CHAPTER 55 225
CHAPTER 10 45	CHAPTER 33 137	CHAPTER 56 229
CHAPTER 11. 49	CHAPTER 34 143	CHAPTER 57 233
CHAPTER 12 53	CHAPTER 35 147	CHAPTER 58 237
CHAPTER 13 57	CHAPTER 36 153	CHAPTER 59 241
CHAPTER 14. 61	CHAPTER 37 157	CHAPTER 60 245
CHAPTER 15. 65	CHAPTER 38 163	CHAPTER 61 247
CHAPTER 16 69	CHAPTER 39 169	CHAPTER 62 253
CHAPTER 17. 71	CHAPTER 40 175	CHAPTER 63 257
CHAPTER 18 77	CHAPTER 41. 179	CHAPTER 64 259
CHAPTER 19 81	CHAPTER 42 183	CHAPTER 65 263
CHAPTER 20 85	CHAPTER 43 187	CHAPTER 66 267
CHAPTER 21 89	CHAPTER 44 191	CHAPTER 67 271
CHAPTER 22 93	CHAPTER 45 195	CHAPTER 68 279
CHAPTER 23 97	CHAPTER 46 197	
CHAPTER 24 103	CHAPTER 47 199	

SECTION THREE: **SEARCHING FOR THE TRUTH**   283

    CHAPTER 69   285

    CHAPTER 70   291

    CHAPTER 71   295

    CHAPTER 72   297

    CHAPTER 73   301

    CHAPTER 74   303

    CHAPTER 75   307

    CHAPTER 76   311

    CHAPTER 77   315

    CHAPTER 78   319

    CHAPTER 79   327

SECTION FOUR: **LIFE AFTER DIAGNOSIS**   333

    CHAPTER 80   335

    CHAPTER 81   339

    CHAPTER 82   345

    CHAPTER 83   349

GALLERY   353

ABOUT THE AUTHOR   361

FOREWORD

JULY 2018

After living our lives in the famous "throw-away society" of the past many years, the idea of friendships that last a lifetime is hard to imagine. Especially when the lifetime in question spans almost 90 years. So, here you have a report on 90 years of a life and 90 years of being there through the good and sad days.

We start with the birth year of 1928 for your author and me. Being raised in a small community of 6,000 people, we were all one family. Combining our community and church lives caused our bond to grow stronger and stronger each year.

Coming to grips with the challenges of our daily lives was not easy. Jackie has not only faced her own challenges; she has overcome them as well.

In her book, *The Habit*, we have the opportunity to see what so many of us refuse to acknowledge. In the early days of Jackie's life, she was confronted with a problem that most of us did not know about or understand.

Before we go forward, there is a story that I would like to share.

The year was 1938-39. The Great Depression was raging all over the United States. Come February, we all started to think of Valentine's Day. We exchanged Valentine's Day cards in our fifth-grade class. I had found one very special valentine with a little girl on the front cover. The little girl had red hair attached to the front of the card. I showed this special treat to all of the little girls in our class. It was the delight and envy of the class. Who would Viga Hall give the valentine to? When the big day arrived, I handed my friend, Jackie, the girl with the red hair, the Valentine's Day card. To this day, I dare say; she remembers that event.

So, it is that life goes, and we work to make the best of it. Surely, we would all agree that the struggles which have faced Jackie have been well-met. It is a wonderful thing to read the story of the life of a woman who suffers from OCD. Even more remarkable, it is the fact that at 90 years of age, she continues to have the mental clarity to produce this excellent work.

It is a great honor and pleasure to say a large thank you to Jackie. I am sure in this day and age, we all know people who suffer from OCD. Perhaps, if we can all share our love and compassion for each other, there will come a time when OCD will be a thing of the past.

Thanks to people like Jackie, we are moving in the right direction.

–VIGA B. HALL, JR.
Northridge, CA

P.S. ONE LAST THOUGHT:

Talked to Jackie and she still has in her possession the valentine of the girl with the red hair.

INTRODUCTION

IN THE 1930S AND 1940S, mental illness was not widely accepted as a reality in America. When I was a child, I developed a mental condition, later called obsessive-compulsive disorder (OCD), due to prior circumstances in my life. I couldn't understand what I was going through. I first noticed it when I was reading the book, *Lorna Doone*. I couldn't understand some of the passages. I would fixate on them and go over and over them in my mind, trying to understand the meaning of the words.

I worried about everything. These worries are called "symptoms" of OCD, I later learned. As I began to realize that something had gone wrong in my mind, I began to sort out systems whereby I could handle the worries and feel safe. But it had to be secretive; I didn't want anyone to think I was crazy.

So, I began to put the worries in a file folder, so to speak, but what to do with the files, each of them containing an unresolved worry? I was only 10 years old, but I had seen file drawers. I decided my arm would be the "file drawer" where I could place the worry files. Then I devised a system where I would blow on my arm at the end of the day, thus eliminating the files with the worries in them. That's how I managed these unwelcome thoughts for a while. But then my parents noticed my peculiar behavior and admonished me for developing such a crude habit. Naturally, I couldn't tell them what I was doing. They wouldn't have understood, and I didn't know how to put it in words. I also didn't want them to think I had completely lost my mind.

Actually, at the time, I didn't think I had lost my mind—I thought I had just developed a bad habit. I would say my prayers each night and ask God to "help me break my habit." Thus, the title of this book. It was important not to let anyone know of my affliction, so I kept the disorder in my mind rather than displaying overt symptoms like washing my hands incessantly or not stepping on a crack in the sidewalk. My obsessions were (and still are) private. The condition made me seem slow to some people like I couldn't follow directions quickly. I couldn't hit a softball, and after two tries at playing golf, I just forgot about it. I couldn't even hit the golf ball. But I was good in school. I usually finished close to the top of the class.

There were other problems. Once, I watched a movie about a serial killer, and for two days wondered if I had killed someone. Other instances made me feel like I was going mad, too. I went to a few different doctors and was put on medications, but I had to keep going back because, at times, the habit to obsess was too strong for the pills. It felt like I had to do a specific thing (whatever my brain dreamed up) to make my world safe. Living with the family I did, who did not have the same mental health challenges as me, meant not only did I not understand why I had a sudden and irresistible urge to understand a sense-less passage or saying, but they had no idea why I acted the way I did either.

As I write this, there have been huge leaps in medical advancements and treating OCD. But when the symptoms first appeared, people didn't trust psychiatrists. Later, when I first consulted a psychiatrist, my husband at the time was suspicious of the supposed care the doctor wanted to give me. People made the comparison that if they weren't sick, if they were able to control their bodies and their minds, then there should be no reason why I couldn't do the same.

But I couldn't. When I convinced myself I had been assaulted, or that all the teachers believed I was cheating, the thoughts just looped in my mind. I couldn't listen to reason, and I was far too embarrassed to tell anyone what I was struggling with because I knew they were different from me. It was exhausting to fight so much at times, to have no control over what I HAD to do to work through an emotion or upsetting event. I had to follow the orders my brain was giving me...even if my brain was broken.

I know now that OCD means people repeat actions because it makes them feel safe. It gives them a sense of control, even when what they are is mostly out of control. One in about 40 adults are diagnosed with OCD in America each year, but back when I was young, I felt like I was the only one who had "thought trouble." That's why I want to share my story.

I want to give people who are suffering with it hope. I want to tell you that you don't need to feel ashamed for requiring medication. You don't need to perceive yourself as broken. Can you imagine what it would be like to go through life unable to resist your urges, and mostly worrying about everything? I can. Wherever I was, I had to listen to what my brain was ordering me to do, even if it was in front of strangers and family and schoolmates, but of course, I did what I could to control myself.

When I couldn't control myself, this resulted in mortifying situations, which I share here with you. Many times, it meant that I became even more withdrawn because I knew something was wrong and I desperately wanted to hide as I was forced just to carry on and go through life. Goodness knows, I constantly tried to make up rules around my OCD. I thought if I resigned myself to handle the compulsions by these rules that I was managing my obsessive compulsions. But I wasn't.

I hope you will enjoy this story of my life, which in addition to explaining my disorder, relates the reality of the Depression era. Take a trip with me to an earlier time when gasoline was so expensive sometimes a family had to sell their car, and when the dynamics between men and women dating were vastly different. Let me tell you about my upbringing with a combined family, and how I discovered I was pregnant and then was married in one week! My life does not resemble the stories that you hear and read about from this time period when women were reserved and dated very few men (and sometimes only one!) before settling down. My adventures kept pace even with the women of today. But as I lived them, I was the outcast because while others were on track to a sensible existence, I wasn't.

My life changed many, many times and all the way through I just tried to do the best I could. Now, I am in my 90s, and my mind is sharp, my memories as vivid as if they occurred yesterday.

Yes, inventions come along, laws change, society progresses, but regardless of the time in which you grew up, people are the same. They want the same love, acceptance, and confirmation that they are as normal as anyone else. And it doesn't matter who's in the White House, what war is waging or where we are in the battle of the sexes. Despite the historical references that I have included in this book, I think there will be times when you are reading that you will forget about the years that have flown by from then to now. Because we are all the same at our base.

If you are reading this and fighting your own habit, the best advice I can give you as one who has survived with and without medication is to get help. You need to tell yourself it's okay that you have this condition. We know about more people living with OCD now, and it is so much easier to get through your days when you have a treatment plan. You don't have to feel alone, like an oddball, or as if no one understands, because OCD is real, and people today know it is a genuine affliction. Since I was a young girl, when something changed in my brain to make me the way I am, I have lived with this disease. If I can do it, you can. Don't do it the way I did, though. Don't deny yourself the care you need to be happy.

It looks like America is on the way to outgrowing the shame of mental illness. It's about time.

You're about to learn about the steps that I took to save my life. I hope it will help you in your journey and that it will reinforce for you why we need to support people when they are sick.

Now, let's travel back in time to 1928.

SECTION ONE

THE
Break

CHAPTER 1

AS OFTEN HAPPENS with mental disturbances, the solution comes unbidden, whether it's the right one or not. I was married when my life unraveled one night and took a new direction that would affect my son and me forever.

It was shortly after New Year's, and my husband, Ward and his mother had gone to a farmers' co-op meeting and left me at home alone with my new baby, Todd, and the yard dog, and it was then that I reached the end of my endurance.

When I could no longer hold back the despair I was feeling about my dysfunctional marriage and the fear I had for the future of my son, I screamed at the top of my voice. It was one of the first screams of such depth that I had ever emitted up to that time in my life. As I had said, I often screamed beneath my voice since there had always been someone around to hear; obviously, I couldn't really let loose.

However, I did that night. Of course, I awakened the baby, and he cried and the dog, bless his heart, thought something drastic had happened. He ran around the house barking to scare off any marauder that might have been there. But as the character Pogo said, "We have found the enemy, and he is us."

I realized I had to get things under control before Ward and Edith returned. Foremost was the fact that I had to comfort my frightened baby. The dog calmed down when he heard nothing more, but I realized the time had come when I had to do something to change my life.

When Ward returned home, I told him I was going to my parents' home the next day and that I was taking Todd. He said, "Why?"

I said, "You surely know I can't live the way we're living any longer. I have to have someone I can depend upon to help me raise our baby."

He asked, "What good will it do you to go there?"

"I don't really know," I said. "And I don't know if I'll ever come back. I just want to go home."

Surprisingly, the next morning, after I had packed my things, as well as supplies for Todd, he took me to be with Mother and Daddy. While they had suspected things weren't going right, they didn't think it had come down to this.

They said to Ward, "You can come to see Jackie and the baby any time you want to."

They also assured him, "We're not taking sides since we don't know what's been going on."

Mother and Daddy were, of course, dismayed that I had come back home, but they welcomed me and asked few questions. They did want to know if I planned ever to go back to Ward. By the end of the first day, my thoughts had crystallized enough to determine that if Ward would get a job and we could move away from his mother's, I would try again. After all, I did love him and our baby and had been happy as a family—of sorts. I felt I could be happy again if I just had some security.

SECTION TWO

Undiagnosed

CHAPTER 2

PERHAPS TO HAVE BEEN BORN in the circumstances in which I arrived would automatically preclude that destiny would not be kind. However, my sister, Billie came along just 17 months later into the same environment as I and her demeanor throughout life was certainly different from mine. She would be considered a virtual success. But there are many factors which go into a person's psyche, no matter how close he or she is to another sibling. Such was our case. I did not perceive life in the same way that Billie did. I'm happy for her sake that she was not like me.

I was born in a little frame house in Mooresville, Missouri which had inside plumbing and heat, though not central. In 1928, quite a few people lived in poverty since this was the beginning of the oppressive Depression, and, as such, many families had to live together. In our case, my mother, Olga, and father, Ralph, who were married in April of 1927, lived in the same house as my paternal grandmother.

I don't know who owned the house—my father or

grandmother—but my mother contended my father did since he had had to support my grandmother after the death of his father when he was only thirteen.

At that time, my grandparents lived on a small non-productive farm west of Perfect, a town of 700 just six miles south of Mooresville. It was strictly a farming area, even if the soil was rough, rocky and hilly. My family was quite poor, although my father's paternal grandfather was purported to have had money. However, since his off-spring squabbled so much over it, he buried it, and it was never found. Or so the legend goes.

Daddy was the youngest of eight children, born when my grandmother, Ma, was about forty-three. It did not oc-cur to me as I was growing up that Ma could have gone to work to support my father and the two grandchildren who lived with her, doing domestic work, if nothing else.

Instead, Daddy had to leave the eighth grade and, since he could hardly work a farm at that tender age, the fam-ily moved to Mooresville where he found a job as a call boy for the railroad. He was a big boy in size and had to lie about his age to get the job. I think the farm may have been sold with Ma using the proceeds to buy the small house in Mooresville.

There were two grandchildren, Morris and Mary, who went along since they were the half-orphaned children of one of Daddy's oldest sisters, Bertha, who had died. I don't know much about their father, and I'm not sure if they even had the same father. Many of those skeletons we didn't even talk about, but I did know that Bertha died while her children were quite young, leaving them in Ma's care and, eventually, to be supported by my father, young though he was.

To be strapped with so much responsibility at such a young age can readily be blamed for any personality characteristic or emotional problems my father might have developed later, some of which were passed onto his own daughters, especially me (or so I thought.) But I cannot fault him for any of the mistakes he might have made as a father. Basically, he was a kind, sweet man, ever forgiving and remorseful for any of his own actions which might have hurt others.

I am not sure how far either Morris or Mary went to school, but they did not graduate from high school. In those days, people weren't too concerned about school dropouts—they were more concerned about having a roof over their head and food on the table. However, by the time my parents married, Morris had already left the home and married Cliffy. Mary was there for a brief time after Morris's marriage but later left to marry Otto, a drunken ne'er-do-well. Of course, Mary beat him up routinely, so he kept pretty much in line when he wasn't drinking.

The household into which I was born in March of 1928 was not necessarily a happy one. My grandmother resented my mother being there, and my mother, a pretty little upstart from the lower hills of the state, was a bit sassy and not accustomed to following the rules. Most of the knowledge about their early life together (i.e., with Ma) has been derived from my mother's angry litany about her problems with Ma. She hated her and did so the rest of her life. I used to question Mother's veracity, but now I'm not so sure that it wasn't as bad as she said.

Mother, referred to Ma as "that thing!" maybe because Ma was jealous of my father and his relationship with my mother. Mother had even gone so far as to state that they were much too close for a mother-son relationship, which

I do not believe. I never saw anything that smacked of intimacy between the two in all my 13 years before Ma died. And my father's conduct with his two daughters was above reproach.

Mother also contended that, when Ma learned she was pregnant with me, Ma "tried to starve me to death and all she would give me were candy bars to eat." Also, according to Mother, Ma persuaded my father not to allow her to get proper medical care.

Mother, it must be told, was a flighty young girl of 17 when she and my father were married in April of 1927. She was quite pretty, never tactful, but intelligent, and at that time without a whit of common sense.

When things went wrong, which they often did, Mother would leave home and go to her parents' house, which was across town in an area called The Hill. She would then wait for my father to come and apologize for whatever wrong he might have done and take her back home.

Mother usually resolved her problems this way—by leaving—and did it for many years of my parents' married life, even as late as when she was in her 70s. In one incident, she must have been in her seventh month of pregnancy when she became angry and tried to leave again. She only went as far as the downtown corner drug store where she fainted from malnutrition since she had on a non-maternity dress and lightweight coat. This was inadequate in cold January weather.

A scene downtown followed with my mother becoming hysterical. In all fairness to her, she was young and in a situation with which she couldn't cope. As she said later, "There were no agencies, courts or laws which dealt with abused women and children at that time and leaving home was the only weapon I had."

Perhaps it was, but I think her example of running away from her problems so badly impressed her two daughters that neither of us used that means of escape in our own marriages. We would rather have remained to settle the matter in a more reasonable way.

* * *

I WAS BORN AT HOME, but a doctor was in attendance. According to my mother, "Ma sure wasn't happy that you came along. She wanted your dad all to herself."

However, in my 13-year-relationship with my grandmother, I never doubted that she loved me. Mother later said that I became Ma's favorite because I resembled my father, with curly red-blonde hair and blue eyes. She wasn't as fond of Billie, who had dark hair and eyes, like those of my mother and her side of the family. Still, I don't remember my grandmother ever showing that she loved Billie less than she did me.

The discord of the family dynamic affected my parents as well. There were many quarrels between them and my mother leaving, which affected me greatly. My first memory of Mother leaving was when she went to nearby Joffa, to see a girlhood friend. It was during the Christmas season; for some reason, there was almost always trouble before or during the holidays between my parents.

At that time, we didn't know about stress or how the Yule season can bring trouble in a relationship. Once, Mother took both Billie and me with her to Joffa. I remember a small boy who had a foot-long, three-inch-diameter stick of peppermint candy which some of the adults urged him to share with the other children. Not knowing how to divide his candy, he merely pounded it on the floor until it broke into many pieces.

The adults thought this was very funny, but I remember being quite depressed and just wanting to go home. This was one of the few times Mother took us with her when she fled. Usually, she just left on her own.

From as far back as I can remember, her leaving had a devastating effect upon me. I felt abandoned, and when I became a little older, I would wonder who was going to take care of us, comb our hair and get us off to school. I was also very embarrassed and did not want the other children or any of the neighbors to know she was gone.

My first memory of one of her absences from home, when I was quite small, was when she returned. We weren't living with Ma then but had rented a two-bedroom house. Mother was all smiles and happy to see us. She said, "Look, I'm home, and I brought you dolls." But when I thought of that incident as I grew older, it seemed to be a poor substitute for care and concern, of which I felt vastly bereft.

CHAPTER 3

CONDITIONS AT HOME IMPROVED after my parents finally moved away from Ma's house. Later, the house burned down, and Ma had to live in a series of low-rent places, many of which did not have running water, inside plumbing or even electricity. Billie and I liked to stay overnight with Ma; she let us sleep late in a big feather mattress and fixed us breakfast in bed.

For whatever reason—my dad's angst or my mother's leaving—I seemed to have been anxiety-ridden from an early age. I was also very shy and quite gullible. One case in point involved an incident with two older girls who were sisters. They lived down the street after we moved from Ma's house.

I was only about three and a half years old when the two sisters took advantage of my young years to tease me. We were outdoors, and they said to me, "If you'll look up at the attic window of the house, there's a snake which lives up there and at certain times of the day he comes to the window with a top hat and cane and dances."

They further said, "If you'll go home and dress up and come back later in the afternoon, we'll show you the snake."

I thought this was really neat, although I don't quite know how I thought that snake could perform.

I ran home and told Mother to dress me up for a "party." (The older girls had told me not to tell my mother about the snake because it was a secret.) So, I took a bath and put on a clean dress and went back after lunch to see the special performance.

When I showed up, the two girls came out and laughed hilariously at my gullibility. They must have thought *this kid is a real do-do.*

Thus, was my first encounter with mean-minded people and my mislaid trust in others. I was very disappointed and embarrassed, but the lesson of deceit did not soak in. Too bad. It would have saved me from some unsavory situations over the years. However, life was interesting. I still would rather look for the good in people before condemning them for the bad. However, I take more time in judging them than I once did.

CHAPTER 4

AFTER BILLIE CAME ALONG, we moved around quite a bit in Mooresville. Our neighborhood was lower middle-class, but certainly a cut above Martin Hill, which was across the railroad tracks and where my maternal grandparents lived.

My mother's father, Robert, was French and had he lived in France, I'm sure he would definitely have been a dashing ladies' man. He liked to dance, sing and play the mandolin; unfortunately, since he would have rather done that than make a living. He came from would-be farmers, but I suspect his forbearers were all of the light-hearted, merry-spirited persuasion that he was rather than being the type to settle down to a serious profession. He did, however, work as a shoe cobbler, but was always starting small shops, that failed before getting more backing (usually from my father) for another one.

I preferred Grandpa to Grandma, but I never did feel very affectionate toward either of them. They weren't nearly as nice to me as Ma was, and I hated to visit them.

So, did Billie. Mother insisted we go at least every other Sunday, despite how much we complained about it.

Their house smelled, for one thing. Granted, this was during the Depression, and while they lived in poverty, they were clean. But on Martin Hill, the poor part of town, sewer facilities weren't always up to par, and Grandma cooked with a kerosene stove which emitted noxious smells of its own.

All of this combined with the pungency of mothballs, plus tobacco juice which Grandma herself emitted from her long-time habit of chewing. Say what you will about that awful habit, she still had most of her teeth when she died at 92, although they were yellowed.

Going to Grandma's and Grandpa's house was something my sister and I balked at constantly. Another reason for our reluctance was because of Margaret, our half-cousin who lived with them. Poor Margaret Tinker was two years older than I, and the daughter of my mother's half-brother, Lawrence, whose wife had died while Margaret was still a baby. So. my grandparents reluctantly took her in. I thought they were terribly harsh with her and she, in turn, was sassy to them.

Sometimes my sympathy for Margaret outranked my dislike of her. She was hateful to Billie and me, probably resulting from jealousy since, even though we weren't privileged, we were better cared for and nurtured than she was. Children can be so cruel, and I'm afraid we were guilty of that toward Margaret most of the time.

Although my grandparents had inside plumbing, Margaret neglected personal hygiene and had an odor. (I wondered if anything or anybody on Martin Hill didn't just absorb that smell through the process of osmosis.) Then, too, Margaret didn't have the advantage of a proper diet and, while not fat or obese, she was overweight. She had the same nice brown hair and eyes with thick lashes that my mother was blessed with, and, with care, could have been pretty.

She went to Martin Hill Elementary School, and there was a general unpleasant smell there, such as I believe is the case for most elementary schools.

After grade school, Margaret also attended the only high school in town where Billie and I were registered. We were reluctant to admit she was our cousin. We did nothing to help her, except on one isolated occasion when I acted with unfamiliar grace, kindness, and honor. Margaret and I were in the same physical education class, and though the other girls made fun of me because I was so inept at sports, they were particularly stinging toward Margaret and jibed her about her name, calling her "Margaret Tinker-Tot."

But Margaret was an excellent soccer player and in one tournament scored magnificently, propelling her team on to victory. Instead of merely yelling their support of her, the other girls couldn't resist the urge to taunt her with "Margaret Tinker-Tot." I thought they were very cruel and, in spite of my shyness and reluctance to irritate others or call negative attention to myself, I got up and yelled, "Leave her alone," then I ran to the dressing room in tears.

Since I had very few friends, no one followed me to see if I was all right or to inquire why I had produced such an outburst. So, I was ignored when the other girls came in to shower, although my gym teacher, Miss Miller, did call me to her office to inquire why I had gotten so upset. I told her Margaret was my cousin and I just felt sorry for her.

She said, "Well, you were justified in feeling the way you did so just forget the embarrassment (about my actions)." I made a small brownie point with Miss Miller that day, and, although I was still a complete klutz in gym, she treated me a little kindlier thereafter.

CHAPTER 5

MY FIRST FIVE YEARS in Mooresville were average, unexciting and probably did not explain the personality changes and problems I was later to encounter. I was a shy child and nearly all my pictures taken at that time show me with a frown.

When my sister came along I think I loved her—I always seem to have—but I probably experienced some sibling rivalry as most young children do when a baby comes into the household. My mother said I took Billie's bottle away from her for myself until she finally gave me a bottle of my own to appease me.

I don't remember much about my parents' relationship at that time, and as best as I can remember, life revolved around Ma. She was always there to give me a comfortable feeling. I don't know how long the forced living arrangements existed, but I think they came to an end when I was about three years old and the house burned down. I remember standing at a window about a block away and seeing the house go up in flames.

I think after that Ma had her own place, certainly not a castle but the best she could afford on her old-age pension and some help from my father. She lived in the same neighborhood as before, but in various low-rental houses.

I was especially impressed by the periods I spent with Ma. I remember her "scraping" apples for Billie and me, which saw her scraping the fruit off with a knife and feeding it bird-like to her two favorite granddaughters. She also fixed crumbled cornbread in a glass of buttermilk, which we thought was a great delicacy.

By kerosene lamplight, she would sing "Old Dan Tucker" in her unmelodic voice. It seemed Old Dan Tucker sang for his supper and "died with a toothache in his heel." Ma definitely had very little talent for singing, but we enjoyed her songs nevertheless.

* * *

MY HAIR WAS CURLY and golden blonde, which I inherited from my father, and much was made over how pretty it was, especially in contrast to Billie's straight brown hair, which I think was quite unfair to her. An old photo shows Billie at about a year and a half in age and me at about three years old, standing on the fender of our dad's car. Billie, whose dark brown hair gleamed in the sunlight, looked so cute and fragile, to compare her unfavorably with me was not kind. And there was plenty of unfair treatment back then.

In those days desegregation did not exist; people were merely racist and thought nothing of it. There were minstrel shows, and we had no blacks living in town or immediately outside the city limits. Although there was not a written law keeping them out, they nevertheless did not try to locate there, especially not after two black men were hanged by vigilantes for the rape and death of a white woman around the turn of the twentieth century. Later, however, it was determined they were innocent, and the perpetrators of the crime were actually white.

I'm sure Ma felt no qualms of conscience when she sang one of our favorite songs— "Run, n*gger, run, the Kuckalucks will catch you; run, n*gger, run, you'd better get away."

I didn't understand that song because I didn't know what Kuckalucks were. It wasn't until I was in high school that it finally dawned on me that she was singing about the Ku Klux Klan.

Ma also regaled us with stories of the Civil War and ghost stories, especially the one about a headless man who drove his wagon on moonlit nights in Corsicana. That story scared us, but what child doesn't like to be scared out of his knickers?

At about this time, when I was almost five, I began to be curious about sex. There were two or three instances that defined this subject for me, one where I walked in on my father after he had just finished bathing and was sitting on the commode drying. He yelled at me, "What are you doing in here? You should know better than to walk in on somebody in the bathroom!" He was very angry, and I didn't know what I had done wrong, but it *must have been pretty bad*, I thought.

Another time, I had gone across the street to visit with two little boys, Kenny and Benny, who were eating vegetable soup. Benny was about three years old and sitting in his high chair when all of a sudden, he announced, "I gotta pee!" His mother told him to go out on the back porch.

Without a word, I went with him so, frankly, I could watch. I had a vague idea about boys' equipment but had never actually seen one at work, and I was curious. No one called after me, but when I went back into the house, Kenny made a remark to the effect that what I had just done was not very nice.

I went home and told my mother, and she treated it as a "sin," but added, "the Lord will forgive you if you don't do it again." I'm not criticizing my mother or her good intentions. This was what she had been taught, so that's what she taught me. Unfortunately, I was a prisoner of my past—all five years of it—so by the time I entered kindergarten, I had built-in guilt already.

The fact that arguments between my parents continued after I entered kindergarten didn't help my adjustment. I was very shy and don't remember speaking up at all. I do remember on the first day a little girl who sat across from me flipped my new box of crayons, so I immediately took a dislike to her and decided friendship with her was not going to be easy.

When I went home, I told my parents, "There was a mean girl, so I'm not going back." They thought differently, of course, but in my mind, I just couldn't deal with it. Naturally, I went back the next day but still didn't have much to say to anyone.

As for the arguments between my parents, I remember a particular one about two months later when my mother went home to Mama again on Marshall Hill and took Billie and me. I was petrified about how I was going to get to school and then get back to Grandma's over those railroad tracks.

Mother told me, "Don't worry. I'll be there to walk with you to school part of the way each morning and meet you on your way home." I insisted I needed her when I crossed the tracks. She sensed my apprehension and said, "I'll pick you up on Third Street about a block and a half away from the school. That way, we can walk over the tracks together."

This fight between my parents may have been minor. I only remember going to and returning to Grandma's once. It was quite a struggle for Mother to have to walk me all the way to school and back. Of course, when I started the trek from school that day, she was late. As I walked down the Third Street hill leading to Main Street and she hadn't arrived, I was devastated. But finally, she turned the corner. I was so relieved, I probably cried.

When mother left the next time, Billie and I did not go with her. For one thing, we didn't want to, as it was very inconvenient and stressful getting us to and from school without an automobile.

Leaving us at home didn't always alleviate the problems—at least not for me. I don't think it bothered Billie so much when Mother left as it did me. I would become a nerve-ridden little person, not knowing who was going to curl our hair, iron our dresses and get us ready to go to school. Ma usually helped out in those instances, so that was some relief.

I must have felt abandoned when Mother took off on her spells of vengeance. Later those feelings of loneliness and being left behind caused me numerous problems. I never quite overcame my strong sense of desperation and abandonment when I was left alone.

CHAPTER 6

THEY SAY LIFE IS A JUNGLE out there; well, it certainly was for me when I was growing up. I must have led a very protective life before going to school because I was ill-prepared to cope with the other youngsters. I was easily hurt or angered, but seldom fought back. I would just sulk, a bad habit that went with me long after I should have left it behind, even up to and including adolescence. I was not a pleasant child and did not talk much.

Sunny Billie, who talked easily, had a lovely dimpled smile and was the outgoing one of the two of us, was quite the opposite. I learned early on to hide behind her skirt and let her lead the way. Although I was older, she ended up actually being my caretaker, especially in affairs dealing with other people.

I joked after I grew up (and old) that I failed childhood. I should have been sent back to the womb, so I could start over.

Fights were common in our neighborhood and were one of the reasons my parents didn't want us to associate with the other kids. Billie usually took the lead when we had to defend ourselves. She could fight along with the rest of them and wasn't afraid. Girls can be as mean as boys, and there were some really tough girls in the neighborhood.

One time, however, I didn't have Billie along to protect me and had a very unpleasant experience. I was about six years old and was walking home from school with Berniece, an unpopular girl who lived close to us.

All the kids knew Berniece, who was quite large for her age and had been adopted. None of us liked her and suspected her adoptive parents didn't like her either. Perhaps they didn't; poor Berniece was even more inept than I was when it came to social graces.

That particular day I was walking alone with her, and I had a large jawbreaker in my mouth which I was enjoying immensely. Berniece said, "Don't you have another one for me?" With my mouth full, I told her I didn't.

Before I knew it, she had stopped me and inserted her thumb and one of her large fingers into my mouth, to get that jawbreaker. I guess she wanted it badly. I screamed and shoved her away, then ran all the way home. I was quite upset, as I guess anyone would be when accosted by a larger person, especially someone already known to be as bad as the troll under the bridge.

My parents were upset as well, and my father went to Berniece's parents' home to tell them what she had done. In no uncertain terms, he said, "Keep your daughter away from my girls." That was the last time she bothered me. If I saw her coming toward me, I immediately crossed the street.

Unfortunately, for the ungainly Berniece, this was not the first of such bizarre incidents and her parents finally threw in the towel, and she was returned to the children's home from whence she came. It was a sad case but who wants someone else's fingers in their mouth unless they're medically qualified to be there? Scared though I was, it didn't pass over me that my parents had taken up for me and were appropriately concerned. *They must love me after all*, I thought.

CHAPTER 7

I THINK I was always considered to be just a little on the dumb side because I was extremely naïve. I was reared with the simple doctrine of good or bad, and I thought if you were good, everyone else would be good to you, that only good fortune would befall you.

I got this from my mother's religious doctrine, and while I felt religion was forced down my throat much too much, I still absorbed a lot of its tenets and have been religious most of my life in one way or another.

I believed devoutly in God, and today don't question what I perceive to be His actions in spite of pain, tragedy and worldwide disasters that we read about every day. I don't know exactly why those things happen, but I don't think God is to blame for everything. If he is, perhaps he's trying to teach us a lesson. Also, perhaps we wouldn't know real happiness if we didn't know of pain; that release from adversity shows us how fortunate we are in our everyday hum-drum life. What I'm saying is, without pain, there is no glory.

With all the mental and psychological problems I experienced throughout life, I have always had moments of extreme happiness. I think adversity increases our capacity to experience great joy. And so, it was with me.

On occasions when I seemed to be unaware of what was going on or just didn't get the point, I absorbed more than others thought I did. I was, admittedly, very naïve and trusting of others to the point I usually believed what they said. In my simple religious training, I thought people were either good or bad, and that the good ones didn't lie.

I have always believed whatever most people told me. I think I still do! In my early years, we attended the Methodist Church, which had its own brand of hell-fire and damnation. I learned that if I wanted to get to heaven, I'd better not sin, so I was very concerned about my wrongdoings at an early age. Incidents that probably would not have bothered others, who didn't have the nagging conscience that I had, were of utmost importance to me.

When I was about six, Ma took me to Maryville, the county seat where her brother-in-law, Uncle Fred, was sheriff. We visited Uncle Fred and his wife, Aunt Maude, who lived in the comfortable sheriff's house for many years since Uncle Fred, a very capable officer, continued to get elected. Aunt Maude cooked for the prisoners who were held in jail at noon each day, which was a part of the job.

One day, Aunt Maude and Ma went to the jail with Uncle Fred around lunchtime to feed the prisoner. I didn't want to go and, as soon as they left, with my growing curiosity getting the best of me, began to explore the house.

Two incidents occurred, one was an adventure, and the other was a personal matter.

The personal matter later bothered me a great deal to the point where I eventually felt compelled to tell my mother. All I did was go into the living room where Aunt Maude had a large, swivel-type, oval wood-framed mirror. I pulled up my dress, pulled down my panties and looked at myself in that mirror. That's all, honest. But I thought I had committed a terrible sin.

The other misdeed was, in my little mind, a crime—I picked up the telephone (we didn't have one at home until I was 13 years old)—and gave a number to the operator. Then I told the startled woman who answered my call that the operator connected, "I just wanted to talk on the telephone and there's nothing you can do about it."

That was a very sassy statement for me. I hurriedly said it to get it over with, but so felt that it was time I learned how to talk on the phone.

I didn't tell Ma or Aunt Maude about my terrible transgressions when they returned. Later, though, I told Billie, and she told my dad about the phone incident. It wasn't Billie's nature, nor mine, to be a tattletale; I think she just told him because she thought it was funny. Daddy thought so, too, and teased me about it. He said, "Did you make a phone call to someone in Maryville?" I reluctantly said yes, and he jokingly told me, "You could have gotten into a lot of trouble for that, and maybe Uncle Fred should have been told."

I didn't think any of this was a bit funny, but Daddy, seeing my discomfort, finally said, "Don't worry. We're not going to mail him a letter and tell him. You really didn't do anything wrong. But don't use the telephone again unless it's really important."

To further illustrate what an uptight little kid I was, or how easily embarrassed I could become, when I was in the first grade, and Billie was in kindergarten, she was invited to a birthday party one Saturday afternoon. That was my day to get my hair washed and curled. Our cousin, Morris (one of the orphaned children Ma raised), took Billie to the party in Daddy's car.

Morris asked me if I wanted to go along, even though I had just had my hair washed and it wasn't dry or even combed. Also, I had on an everyday dress and was wearing my Mary Jane shoes with my toes over the toe-end of the shoes, sandal-style. Billie and I were ingenious, to say the least—when we didn't have what we wanted, like sandals, we made our own.

But the funny part—at least for the others—came when Morris arrived with us to the party and the birthday girl's mother walked out to the car to accompany Billie to the backyard. When she saw me, she urged Morris to let me stay also. I really should not have, knowing how embarrassed I was about my wet, kinky hair, old dress, and pseudo-sandal shoes, but I agreed anyway and joined the doings.

I was not the belle of the ball by a long shot. The other kids remarked about my wet hair, and one little girl took great delight in pointing out the funny way I was wearing my shoes. Had I been more secure, perhaps not so shy, or even a little smarter, I would have thought it was funny also, but, true to form, I was miserable and didn't take part in the party at all.

The best I felt the entire afternoon was when Morris

came to pick us up and I thought I had committed a faux pas. In retrospect, I was a little hard on myself about the entire incident. I was only six and what kid that age can make good decisions?

But the one time I really pulled the faux pas was when I was older and should have known better. Had I let my shyness come to the fore on that occasion and stay there (where it belonged as it turned out), I would not have embarrassed myself or my parents so much.

As I stated, my father worked for the railroad as a caller, and he became acquainted with all the railroad employees and was very well liked. He was even friends with the upper echelon of engineers and conductors. One couple, in particular, Mr. and Mrs. Miller, who had no children of their own, had seen Billie and me with our father and took a great deal of interest in us.

I must admit, we were cute, being the opposite of each other in our coloring, yet the same size. Mother kept us dressed in pretty dresses which she made for us, usually designed after Shirley Temple's frocks. They were often alike but in different colors.

The Millers asked Daddy and Mother to bring us over to their house one day when I was about seven years old and Billie, six; they had a gift for us. When we arrived, they handed us a swan cradle-like, long chair-seat holding five little baby dolls, replicas of the Dionne Quintuplets (the first surviving quintuplets). The small dolls were quite lovely; all had on different pastel-colored pique rompers and bonnets, and little white shoes and socks. Also, each of them had a tiny necklace around her neck with her name inscribed upon it.

Billie and I were enchanted, and since I was the oldest, the Millers handed the gift to me. Then Mother and Daddy urged, "What do you say now?" and, for want of something better to say, I said, "How much did it cost?"

I'm sure Mother and Daddy would gladly have slithered under the Miller's couch, and I could tell from their actions that I'd blown it...big time. I think the Millers had enough of a sense of humor to laugh, and that was not the last gift they gave us. I'm sure they realized I received a lesson in proper etiquette when I returned home.

Fortunately, I haven't done that again; I hesitate to ask the price of anything now, even the daily specials at a restaurant.

CHAPTER 8

I WAS AN ODD KID, but I was always very serious-minded. However, I was also thoughtful of others in small ways. I wasn't altogether selfish and didn't mind sharing.

Once, when I was about four years old, I was lying on the floor with Betty Jo, an older girl from up the street who was very blonde. I was aware that others considered my hair to be pretty with its curls and reddish color, so I said to Betty Jo, whose hair was neither curly nor full, "Why don't I pull out some of my hair and put it in yours, so it'll grow back curly like mine? That way, your hair can be pretty, too." Profoundly tactless, but I meant well.

We were with Ma, and she told me, "No, that won't work. You have to be born with curly hair." But she later told my parents that she thought "there's something odd about Jackie. She's too serious. You're going to have trouble with her later."

And I guess they did. Even if they didn't, I certainly had trouble with ME. So did Ma, but she was more patient with me than Mother and Daddy were.

Ma played an important part in our lives as Billie and I were growing up. We came to depend upon her when there was turmoil or quarreling in our home. I don't know if she was just putting on a good act for us to substantiate the fact that the trouble with Mother was all Mother's fault. Anyway, I don't remember Ma ever raising her voice to my mother or hearing the two of them argue.

My mother often said, "Ma just waits for your dad to come home so she can complain about me in private."

I saw no indications of this, but I'm sure there was bad blood between the two of them. Even after Ma had moved to her own house when I was small, she came back at intervals to live with us. Since she was subsisting on her pension for the aged, she didn't have many resources on which to fall back.

However, she did give Billie and me $5.00 a month each for our spending money. She knew, of course, that my dad didn't earn much money and, since we were her favorite grandchildren, she wanted us to have the money.

Probably another benefit for her was the fact that we had a penchant for the movies. However, since our parents wouldn't let us attend at night without an adult, she was elected to go along with us during our grade school years.

She enjoyed the movies also and would gladly sit on the front row with us, craning her neck as we did to look up at the screen. It must have been very uncomfortable for her. It was for us until we finally realized we would be more comfortable several rows back.

Ma also liked popcorn, but I don't know how she was able to eat it since she had no teeth. As far as I know, she had never even had a set of dentures. I guess she just gummed it.

Poor Ma—Billie and I were really cruel to her. She had a limp resulting from a leg fracture many years before and couldn't walk at a fast clip. On the way home from the movies, about six blocks away, Billie and I would grab her arms and hurry her along since we didn't want to walk so slowly. I'm happy to say we didn't do this often but am ashamed to say we did it at all.

Ma would complain and say, "I hope when you kids grow up you have grandchildren who'll treat you as mean as you do me."

But Ma was not altogether innocent or perfect. For one thing, she didn't like to wear underwear. This didn't apply to petticoats of which she wore several long, flannel ones, even in the summer, but she didn't like panties. She didn't own a pair and thought they were just a nuisance. She also didn't wear a brassiere, and as seldom as she saw a doctor, I suppose she was never told it would be beneficial for her posture and her health to wear one.

Ma's desire not to wear panties didn't bother us except for one thing—when she needed to urinate, she thought nothing of stopping in her tracks (at night, of course) and relieving herself while still standing. We thought that was terrible; however, she didn't do it in the presence of other kids, just us.

I'm sure she had mud on her shoes, but we didn't tell on her, much the same as she didn't tell that we were causing her a great deal of discomfort by expecting her to "hurry up" on the way home from the movies.

So, Ma accompanied us to the movies until I was in junior high school when our parents felt we were old enough to take care of ourselves.

However, in one week we saw all the features: five total. That cost us 50 cents apiece for the week, and Ma, $1.25. I remember our favorite movie for the entire week was "Lord Jeff" with Freddie Bartholomew and Mickey Rooney. All the girls were in love with Freddie, Billie and me among them.

Ma, I might add, was popular with the neighborhood kids on these occasions; they wished they had a grandmother like ours. Incidentally, along with Ma's unabashed immodesty, she had another fault—she smoked a pipe. She paid for her own "terbacky" and tamped it in her corncob pipe along with the best of the smokers.

The loose tobacco in Ma's container, which I think was a discarded round, cornmeal box, was a boon to Billie and me. We liked to roll our own cigarettes, using toilet tissue, and smoking them. Of course, Mother didn't know of that either (Ma was good at keeping secrets) until one day I burned a hole in a good dress and Mother recognized it immediately as a burn when she ironed it.

CHAPTER 9

IN SPITE OF THE FACT that my parents quarreled often, and there was constant friction between my mother and Ma, Billie and I really had a good childhood. Even though we didn't have all the advantages of some children whose family income was greater than ours, we didn't feel underprivileged.

Mother wanted us to learn the piano, but we couldn't afford a piano, so she sent us for dance lessons. And while our clothes were homemade for the most part, they were stylish and pretty. Mother, who had never had a sewing lesson in her life, was an excellent seamstress, and all she needed was a picture to make a garment.

The fact that we were so close in age, brought us closer together. I always considered Billie my best friend and helpmate, and, fortunately, we shared the same sense of humor.

Sometimes humor can get you through the rough spots. While my father was not particularly cheerful when he was young, my mother was and, in her perky way, kept the spirits of the family high. She always looked on the bright side.

One thing we never discussed with each other was sex. Even as close as we were, there's a line you just don't cross.

But we did have fun, even in simple ways. One time when I was about ten years old and Billie nine, Daddy brought home some metal slugs. I don't know what they were used for: pay telephones, maybe. Anyway, to us they looked like real coins and being the movie buffs that we were from an early age, we had seen many slot machines on the screen, though none in real life.

Naturally, the thing to do with the coins was to build a slot machine with which to use them. So, with a little bit of cardboard, adhesive tape (we didn't have cellophane tape at that time), string, and lots of imagination, we made our own slot machine. It worked, too. By pulling a string, some of the coins would roll down a chute. We didn't have a television set for entertainment—we made our own fun.

We learned from all those movies we attended about style and design. We had paper dolls from Shirley Temple to Scarlet O'Hara, but the ones we enjoyed most were some copies of Jane Arden which were simply posed, allowing us to easily draw clothing for them. I still have the crayon-colored, hand-drawn dresses and costumes we made as one of our chief forms of entertainment while still in grade school.

We'd attend a Betty Grable or Alice Faye Technicolor musical, then rush home and draw all the dresses for our paper dolls. We even designed our own and sometimes, after we grew older, we designed dresses for our mother to make for us. Which she did; she could make anything from a picture and a basic pattern.

I think both Billie and I had artistic talent but no art training, and both of us possessed creative minds. Today's kids don't have to think—television and computers do that for them.

Many of my contemporaries remember listening to the radio during our growing-up years, much as we would watch television today. We would sit and listen to "The Creaking Door," "I Love a Mystery" or the weekly dramas on the radio, conjuring up the images in our minds, much as if we were at the movies. I think children had more fun back then. It was a simpler, gentler way of life.

CHAPTER 10

THEN SEX REARED its ugly head.

One day, while I was home recovering from the measles, I wanted to cook something. I was 10 years old but knew how to cook a little. So, I pulled out Mother's recipe box (actually a shoe box) and was looking for a recipe for peanut butter cookies.

Mother wasn't paying much attention to me, but I wish she had been to have circumvented what I found and read. It was porno of the worst ilk, and to this day I don't think that I've ever seen any worse.

It was a little orange-covered book held together with a large safety pin and showed the whole enchilada of sex: masturbation, lesbianism, cunnilingus, fellatio, bestiality, and sex in various positions, and child porn. It was fairly well drawn, in cartoon-form and featured Popeye, Wimpy and Little Annie Rooney and her dog, Zero. The perpetrator of most of the sexual escapades depicted was a French maid named, Fifi. This book was vile; erotic to the nth degree, and arousing.

At 10 years old, I scarcely understood what was depicted on the pages but, having a curious mind and good imagination, I read the entire book and comprehended some of it. Up until that time, I didn't know where babies came from, nor did I know what the F-word meant. It didn't take much, to figure it out.

I was shocked but read it anyway. And I didn't mention it to Mother. I knew she would be frustrated and probably angry with me. I also didn't feel like a religious lecture at that time, so I tucked it away in the bottom of the box. I never saw it again but can remember in detail what was on most of the pages. Needless to say, I didn't bake the cookies; I didn't feel up to it.

I actually told no one. I thought I would be punished if my parents knew I had read the book; I also felt very guilty because it fascinated me so. And I likely felt some arousal, though I didn't know what that feeling was. I couldn't even discuss it with Ma, who was living with us at the time.

But the knowledge and attendant guilt were too much to bear. I had come across the book in April, and by June it had greatly festered in my mind. One night, I heard my parents in the next room having sex. I hadn't known what the real meaning of the sound was, (though I'd had my suspicions) before I read the book.

I began to cry, and Ma wanted to know what was wrong with me. I tried to tell her but couldn't make myself clear. I was very confused about the book—where the maid Fifi had pubic hair; I thought it looked "like a jelly-like substance." (I had never seen a woman's pubic hair before.) But that didn't help Ma in consoling me. She didn't know what I was talking about.

My father, who was of course, still awake and had to go

to work at midnight, came into the room to see what was wrong with me. All I could say was that "I found a little orange book in the cooking box." He was indignant and angry with me admonishing, "You've kept me awake all this time. Now stop your foolishness and go to sleep."

With that, he stomped out of the bedroom and went back to bed. I stopped crying but felt I had done something wrong, so didn't mention the book again until years later. And then not to my parents.

It didn't take me long to realize that babies also came from "the big F," and it was difficult for me to comprehend that grown-ups did "that" in order to have a baby. I thought it was really an enormous sin. It was certainly portrayed as something really bad in the little book, so how could it be explained that even "preachers" did it when they were supposed to be disciples of God?

Eventually, I let Ma know that I knew how babies were made, and it was up to her to explain how they came out of a woman's body. Then I asked her if "doing it" was a great sin, and did "preachers and the president even do it?"

Ma answered as best she could, but it wasn't something she wanted to discuss with a troubled 10-year-old who knew more than she should have at that time. Perhaps the crux wasn't just in knowing but to have learned of it in such a damaging manner. I didn't make it clear to Ma, either, that I had learned all of this from that vile little book.

Naturally, I didn't tell my mother; it was HER book. And I wouldn't have dared tell my father, not after I had already angered him, but also because he was a man. Men in the book were depicted as evil. Women didn't come off well, either, so you can imagine that I lost faith in Mother and Daddy as decent parents right then. It took me a long time to think of them as "good" parents again.

It was a deep mystery to me why they should have such a book around. I thought they must be evil, too, and it wasn't until one of my doctors, when I was grown explained that my mother was young and probably inexperienced when they were first married (she was only 17). My dad might have brought home the book to help arouse her in their sexual life. That made sense to me.

So, it was up to Ma to explain the birds and the bees as best she could, whereupon I definitely vowed that I didn't want to have any babies after I grew up. When I told her that, she said, "Oh, you'll meet a nice young man and get married, then you'll feel different." But I assured her if I even got married, I would just have an agreement with my husband that I wasn't going to do "that" and he would have to understand.

CHAPTER 11

I FERVENTLY BELIEVED that for me there would be abstinence from sex, or I would just never get married. But anything about the subject or the Big-F upset me, and I began crying a lot. I went further into my shell around the other kids and became very distant toward my father. I didn't want him to touch me at all, as though if he did it, it would be an act of intimacy.

Also, when I helped my mother with the laundry by hanging out clothes, I was always careful never to let any of my garments touch my father's shirts or especially underwear on the line.

I began having problems in school and was afraid of both my parents, but never Ma. She was my protector; I felt I could talk to her, even just a little, about the things that bothered me. But she couldn't be in school with me, and it was there that I seemed to make bad choices.

One day in class we were given an exam. I was always a good student and did well in my grades, so one of the other girls, Naomi, who sat close to me, whispered to ask me the answer to a question. When I replied that I couldn't tell her, that it would be cheating, she said, "You'd better tell me, or I'll tell something bad I know on your dad."

My father didn't rate very high in my biased evaluation of him at that time, so I felt that whatever Naomi knew must be pretty bad. Although it was an out-and-out case of blackmail, I told her the answer, anyway.

When it came time to grade the papers, our teacher, Miss Ramsey, handed them out to us to do the grading and I received Naomi's. I was very angry with her, though no one knew I was, and I resented the fact that she answered the question for which I had supplied the answer correctly. So, I wrote in very light red pencil "Cheater" on the back of her paper.

Naomi was pretty brassy to have shown this to the teacher who called me to her desk and asked what the situation was all about. I told her what Naomi had said, so she marked through "Cheater" and sent me back to my desk but kept Naomi after school. I think Miss Ramsey should have given me some words of encouragement about the matter, so I could at least have discussed it with her. Instead, she said nothing, which led me to believe I had done something awful, too. This didn't help my already guilt-filled little mind.

Then another incident occurred. Mother often packed lunches for Billie and me but we liked to walk the nine blocks home for a hot lunch while we were in grade school. That is, except on wintery, bad days. At Smith's, we could charge two slices each of cheese and bologna, a loaf of bread and small packages of potato chips to take back to school, which was only a block and a half away.

We had been doing that for quite some time but one

particularly blustery, cold day, I went to the store to buy my lunch to take back to school. For some reason, Billie didn't go with me; perhaps she was ill and home that day.

However, without someone telling me what to do, which I probably really wanted and needed, I thought perhaps I had done something wrong and should call my mother to tell her why I hadn't come home for lunch.

As I related earlier, we didn't have a telephone at home until I was 13, but in emergencies, we called the Alreds, who lived half a block up the street. They would then get one of our parents to come to the phone. I called them that day and Ray, the father, who was a big man and of whom I was afraid since I had seen him being quite harsh toward his own children, answered the phone and went after Mother. He walked all the way up the street and brought her back, and all I wanted to do was tell her I wasn't coming home for lunch.

Mother was quite embarrassed in front of the Alreds, I'm sure, and apologized for my irresponsible action. I knew I had done something wrong then and am sure I was thinking about it all the time I sat with that phone in my hand, waiting for my mother. But in my confused mind at the time, I just decided not to think about it and wait to see what my punishment would be when I returned home after school.

Actually, my parents were confused about why I had done something so foolish, but my only explanation was that I was scared. They reprimanded me and told me not to do it again. My ability to use good judgment seemed to be greatly impaired.

Then I did something else that was far worse, and which later troubled me much more than the embarrassment of the telephone incident.

CHAPTER 12

MY PARENTS AND ANOTHER COUPLE, June and Chuck Lawson, went nightclubbing together for a period of about two years and would leave their two children, Betty, who was Billie's age, and Bobby, who was a year younger, with Ma. Ma was also in charge of Billie and me, and I don't think she even got paid for her effort.

We liked the Lawson kids and always had a great deal of fun when our parents went out. For me it was like a respite—I knew Ma was far less strict than either of my parents, and I could get away with just a little more mischief while they were out. This particular mischief at the age of 11 even shocked one of my psychiatrists years later and troubled me for quite a while afterward.

It was a cold, snowy Saturday in February. The Lawsons and my parents went out, leaving all four kids in charge of Ma at the Lawsons' house. The grown-ups usually didn't come home until the wee hours of the morning, so Ma made us go to bed before they returned, even though we were allowed to stay up later than usual.

That particular night, Ma and all four of us piled into one bed because it was cold. While Bobby was only about nine years old, he had interesting ideas. He nuzzled close to me, and soon we were beneath the covers, at the foot of the bed. There was touching and some bodily kissing where there shouldn't have been. I think Ma knew of this, but she said nothing. Our indiscretion was allowed to continue for a short while, but nothing was ever said about it.

However, it bothered me, not immediately afterward, but within a couple of months. I thought about what I had been a party to and wondered, how, considering that sex scared and repelled me so in the first place, could I have done that? I also became very distant from Bobby and would scarcely have anything to do with him: I wouldn't sit by him on the couch or at the table and would never touch him.

The incident was becoming what I termed "thought trouble." In other words, I was having problems keeping my thoughts under control and avoiding the things that upset me. At the crucial age of 11, I was becoming a first-class worrier. I worried about everything, especially my soul, which I was sure was going to Hell.

As many mental patients know, somehow in the upheaval of our mind, we manage to find respite. We become obsessed about worries, but we usually devise systems whereby we can be relieved of some of the stress.

My saving grace at first was a complicated set of "memory cards" with the particular worries I had about sex, hell and sinning recorded on the imaginary cards, which, in my mind, were filed along my arm. All I had to do with these worries was record them, file them (on my arm), and then blow on my arm and they would go away.

Evolving from all my worries at that time was what I termed as my "habit" aka my unnatural worries. At night I would ask God to please help me "get over my habit." I guess when we get right down to it, the mental process can simply be described as habits, good or bad, in which our thinking develops. Unfortunately for me, I had "bad" habits.

CHAPTER 13

MY FRAME OF MIND when I was 11 years old and in the sixth grade was such that I did foolish, unthinkable things. For instance, one day we had an exam in social studies. I sat on the far wall from our teacher's, Miss Andrews, desk and, for some reason that I can't explain now, after answering the first written question, I opened my Social Studies book and looked up the answer for the second question.

One of the boys in the class, J.L., who sat in front of me, turned around and said, "You'd better not do that." But I continued to derive all of my answers from the book. I was sure Miss Andrews knew what I was doing. However, since she said nothing, I deducted she probably didn't mind, so I just continued looking up the answers. I offered to give them to J.L., but he would have nothing to do with me.

I knew I was doing something wrong, yet since no voice of authority had rebuked me, I rationalized it was OK. The next day, however, Miss Andrews announced to the class, which I thought was rather crass of her, "Some students cheated yesterday on their exam, and will have to take another test to make up for it."

Naturally, Miss Andrews called me to her desk for a private conference. She also she sent a note home to my parents. They had to reply in writing, so she would know they had received it. Mother and Daddy were both angry and concerned that I had done such a thing, and all I could say when asked "why?" was that "I don't know."

I really didn't know. I had always been taught that cheating was a sin. And I probably knew the answers to the questions anyway.

I was even more careful after that incident to keep out of trouble, and not get Mother and Daddy, or my teacher, angry. But one day fate dealt me another blow I couldn't handle well.

We used bottled ink in those days, so I had an inkwell on my desk. I inadvertently didn't screw the top on correctly—it was crooked and at an angle—and I spilled a good amount of ink on one of my school texts. It belonged to the school and stained one corner of the book and most of the pages.

I took the book right away to Miss Andrews and told her "My parents will pay for this, but they'll be angry with me for being so careless." So, I halfway pleaded with her, "I hope the amount isn't very much or they can't, or won't, pay for it."

Of course, this was not true. We certainly had money to pay for a book, but I was quite frightened. Miss Andrews said, "It will just be a quarter or so, so don't worry about it."

Had my parents known that I had almost groveled for sympathy, they would have been very upset. As it was, they didn't know all the details, and I was even more determined not to screw up anymore.

The spilled ink incident pointed out to me that I was not only careless, but pretty dumb to have allowed a thing of such magnitude (in my mind) to occur, and that I'd better be on my guard or I'd get into more trouble.

And I did get into more trouble.

A couple of weeks later, one girl in the class had a birthday and was celebrating with a skating party at a local roller rink, followed by cake and ice cream.

Another of the girls in our neighborhood, Vonna, had been skating merrily along but had fallen. Somehow, her skate came off and hit her in the mouth, demolishing her front teeth.

My parents, ever fearful the same fate would befall their daughters, had already issued the dictum that Billie and I were not to go to the skating rink anymore for fear of losing our teeth. This was met with great concern, much crying, and nagging to persuade them to change their minds.

So, when the invitation for the skating party came up, I finally prevailed upon them to allow me to go. They did, but told me, "Be extra-careful and don't get your teeth knocked out."

I have found in later years that when I tend to get upset, that's when the "habit" or "thought trouble" kicks in. It did that day. While I should have been looking forward to the party, I was apprehensive that I would do something wrong again, and this time I focused on the ink bottle problem.

Since my disaster of a few weeks prior, I was extremely careful to see that the top of the bottle was screwed on securely. I did that every day at the close of school, whether I'd used the ink bottle or not. This particular day I went through the same process, then left for the party.

But I couldn't dismiss the thought that I might not have tightened the lid, that the ink would spill, and I'd be in trouble again. This bothered me at the party, and I became very upset. I was not having any fun.

One teacher, serving as chaperone called me over and asked, "Is there anything wrong? You seem to be worried about something." I assured her there was nothing, and I couldn't have told her what the truth was; she would have thought I was crazy.

I decided right then I'd better put that thought on the back burner and forget it. I tried hard to forget and couldn't even use my "index card" system. I managed to put the fear in the back of my mind and muddled through. But I realized I would have to be more cautious in the future or people would know about my habit and think I was losing my mind. I thought I was.

I was gradually becoming unglued.

I began delegating my worries to the back of my mind, and not thinking of them any more than I had to. That eased some of the worry for me, though I was certainly not functioning at my best. I began to hide my feelings quite successfully, and I settled down into a comfortable niche.

Never having been a really friendly child, I began to be even more unpopular. I had no sense of confidence and relied on others too much to build up my ego. People don't want to do that, especially kids when they're fighting uphill battles to build up their self-esteem.

CHAPTER 14

I WENT INTO JUNIOR HIGH as a seventh grader, at a disadvantage. I had few friends except the mean Sylvia from our neighborhood, who was also a seventh grader. At about that time, the two of us became friendly with a cute little girl, Jeanie, who lived about three blocks from us. But Sylvia was very adept at playing Jeanie and me against each other. When Jeanie and I were at odds, Sylvia always managed to present herself as the best friend of each of us.

I've read that girls in their early years of puberty are especially cruel and devious. It's like they're going through an early menopause when their genes go haywire, and they become little devils. That was Sylvia to the core. She was happiest when she was plotting against someone or causing friction. I noticed she took real pleasure in siding with Jeanie, the both of them directing their venom toward me.

Saturday afternoon was movie matinee day (Ma had been excluded from this activity long before, but I could have used her help.) Sylvia, Jeanie and I met at the theatre almost every Saturday afternoon for the western flick, or sometimes we would meet at each other's home and go from there.

I began to notice they would tell me where to meet them, then wouldn't show up, but would go on to the theatre without me. This upset and hurt me a great deal. Of course, I complained, to no avail, and then continued to allow them to heap such indignities upon me.

My parents were quite concerned that I forgave them for their dastardly deeds, and often told me, "Why don't you drop those girls? There are nicer girls to be with. Sylvia and Jeanie seem to like to hurt you."

But the more they urged me to drop them, the more determined I was that I wouldn't. Actually, with my low self-esteem, I needed them, not to be mean to me, but to grace me with their favors.

One cold Saturday afternoon we attended the movie, and when I left my seat to go to the restroom, Sylvia and Jeanie hid my coat.

My first thought was that my parents would be angry with me for losing it. I implored both girls, "Don't you know what happened to my coat?"

Of course, they insisted they didn't know where it was, but I knew all the time that they did.

After about half an hour of this torture, I began to cry. That must have been the result they wanted, so they said, "Here's your coat. We didn't know you were such a crybaby."

That should have been the beginning of the end, but the end was a long time in coming.

In addition to the stress of Sylvia's and Jeanie's meanness toward me, at the same time, I was experiencing more "thought trouble." I was far more aware of my thinking processes than I should have been since I didn't understand them, nor did anyone else who I could turn to. I simply thought I had a bad habit, added to the fact that I had so little self-confidence. I questioned my urges to take action or to make decisions when I did have enough courage to do them.

I did as my parents told me but questioned their ability to make wise decisions for me. I thought they didn't like anything about me or what I did. Now, I think I misjudged them.

The fact that I made good grades in school is not only amazing, given my frame of mind, but doing so helped me bond to my parents since they were obviously proud. They didn't understand a difficult adolescent. But who does?

My good grades did not bode well with Sylvia especially who was an average-to-low student. One day after a difficult English test, the subject I usually excelled in, Sylvia and Jeanie asked what I had made on the test. Being truthful, I shyly told them I received an "A."

Sylvia got puffed up over that and snarled to Jeanie, "See, I told you she'd say that." My inferior ego wanted to apologize, but I didn't know how, so I said nothing.

Despite my good grades, I did have blocks in reading.

This symptom showed up when I was reading the book, *Lorna Doone*. I noticed I had a lot of difficulty concentrating. I would read the same sentence over and over again but just couldn't comprehend what was on the written page.

I didn't want to tell anyone about this; I was afraid they would put me in the nut house. What good would it have done, anyway? Who had ever heard of a psychiatrist in our little town in the middle of a sparsely developed area?

CHAPTER 15

SINCE MOORESVILLE had a junior college for would-be elementary teachers, and the college was on the third floor of the high school, the system offered student teaching possibilities. These young people could teach in elementary or one-room rural schools with only a two-year college degree, with the understanding they would complete their education during summer vacations.

I had two classes with student teachers, but, alas, both of them were male. Since I was still in the midst of disliking men, I tried to stay away from them. I had the notion that if I got too close, they would take their "thing" out and poke me with it, or just show it to me. I was afraid I'd crumple into a screaming mess on the floor.

So, I just avoided touching any part of them if I could. If I had to approach their desk, I would stand as far away as possible. I didn't even want to breathe the same air they did.

Of our two teachers, I could tolerate one more than the other. He was a slight young man who wore glasses, and I guess this fact made him less threatening. But the other student teacher had a pock-marked face and wasn't very good looking, so I was sure he was one of the bad guys. I dreaded the days he was in my class.

While I had this aversion to the male species, I do realize that 12- and 13-year-old girls aren't especially interested in boys but are more likely to want to please their female contemporaries. Still, I was much too constrained around them and carried it to the extreme even in church

We attended the First Christian church, and young people were expected to embrace their religion and be baptized when they were 12 or 13, much as in other religions when children reach the age of puberty.

Our minister, Rev. Cobb, was quite old. He was a tall man and a big man. I couldn't see getting into the same water in that baptismal tub with him and then having him hold me while I was baptized. I wasn't afraid of water since I could swim, but I was afraid of what might happen in that water.

So, I refused to join the church when the other kids my age did. I told my parents, and anyone else who asked, "I'm just not ready." I was afraid they would think I was nutty if I told them I didn't want Rev. Cobb holding me.

Fortunately, my parents left me alone for the most part, but would obviously have been happy had I gone into the church at the same time Billie did the next year. I didn't go for baptism until I was 15.

Of course, by then I was sure I was going to Hell for not being baptized, but I had overcome my aversion to the Good Reverend somewhat. Having a boyfriend helped.

But I'm not ready to get into the complicated subject of boyfriends just yet. I had to suffer a lot more before I got around to them.

CHAPTER 16

HOWEVER, I will digress. There was Bobby Graham the summer between the sixth and seventh grades. And while I professed not to like boys, men, or anyone in-between since I was afraid of the male species in general, I did, manage to get myself involved with them in ways I later regretted.

Bobby was a nice-looking kid—dark olive skin, brown eyes and hair from his Latin-blooded mother—and a couple of years older than me. His parents and mine had been friends a long time.

The elder Grahams were circus people and traveled throughout the country with their small show. The kids went with them except for occasional attempts at attending regular school, which never seemed to work. Beulah Graham preferred teaching her three kids herself. (There were two older girls, Nedra and Marie.)

At any rate, that particular summer the Grahams were in the area with their circus, appearing at the county fair. One day they came to our house for lunch and to spend the afternoon before returning to Clarksville, for their evening performance. Bobby Graham, Billie, Betty Ann Clark (a neighborhood friend of little significance), and Sylvia, and I were sitting on the screened-in back porch when someone suggested, "Let's play hide and seek."

That sounded innocent, or so we all thought. Somehow, Bobby and I wound up in the same clothes closet as our hiding place, and the first thing I knew, Bobby had his arm around my shoulders. Then, horror of horrors, I felt his little private part rub against my upper thigh in a suggestive manner. I immediately fled from the closet but felt I had really done something wrong that time.

I blamed myself for leading him on. Bobby, being two years older than I, and cavorting around circus-type people, was no doubt more knowledgeable about such matters as sex and girls than I was, and I probably wasn't his first encounter.

I didn't consider myself the type of girl who would even attract boys. The fact that he had come on to me in such a manner brought on great feelings of guilt and concern in the months to come. I considered Bobby Graham, a "naughty boy" and, in later years, when I was obsessed with guilt, I even tore up a photo of him with his two sisters that was in the family photo album. I didn't want to be reminded of that day. Anything that smacked of sex at all frightened me.

Now that I can reflect on the situation without pangs of guilt, I must say he had a lot of audacity to think his little weenie, which couldn't have been more three inches long, would even titillate me.

CHAPTER 17

IN ALL THOSE YEARS of thought troubles and symptoms, I don't think I ever missed a day's work or school, or had a bad nervous breakdown, from my illness. But when I was 13, I came close to having my first.

That was the summer of my malcontent, the summer of the empty house next door, and when my condition worsened.

Mother had angered the neighborhood kids by ordering them to get out of the empty house next door. Naturally, they turned their anger at her toward Billie and me.

Of course, Sylvia was in on it, even though she had put up the façade of being my friend.

Not only did those kids ignore us, they would hide behind trees or bushes or garages, whatever was handy, to pounce out for the purpose of embattlement. We weren't little children and should have been mature enough not to engage in fisticuffs—especially being girls—but that was the tactic they used.

I usually ran from them, but one day, Billie refused to run and took on two of the meaner perpetrators, Erin and Betty Ann. After she properly clobbered both of them, they left us alone.

But that didn't settle my shaken nerves. I had trouble sleeping at night, and the serenity of my world was disrupted. I began to worry about what those kids would do or say to us next. However, being the softie that I was, I tried to whitewash everything to convince myself that things weren't as bad as they seemed. I just couldn't stand a state of all-out war.

As I prayed, I told myself that "every thing is just fine." But I knew everything was not just fine and, try as I would, I couldn't convince myself. Then, to my amazement and discouragement, when I thought about those words, I found I couldn't get a clear picture of what they meant. I didn't know what "every thing is just fine" meant.

I became obsessed with the phrase, and, though I told myself over and over that "every thing is just fine," (separating "everything" into two words, maybe for emphasis?) I couldn't understand or comprehend it. I just went over and over the phrase, much the same as when I read *Lorna Doone*.

The specter of "everything is just fine" seeped further and further into my troubled mind. I could not say those five words without a great deal of mental anguish. So, I began referring to them as "The Five." That way I could identify it without actually having to say it.

If I said the phrase and opened up the fester in my mind,

I would have to think about it and try again, futilely, to get it right. If I didn't, it would drive me to a silent scream. Do you know you can scream silently? I've done it many times; only later as my mental disorder progressed, and I became a little braver, did I emit actual screams when the thoughts got too severe.

Anyone familiar with obsessive-compulsive disorder knows that part of its manifestation is that thoughts will not go away. They have to be dealt with right then and now. Otherwise, how do you go on living?

Well, I went on living, but not functioning well. I was half-there, and my mind was recessed into the depths of mental torture.

One night, I went into the living room and Mother, sensing that something was wrong, asked me, "What's troubling you Jackie? You haven't been yourself lately."

I thought if I told her about Billy Lawson and Bobby Graham and looking at my nudity in the mirror when I was six, plus some of the other "sins" I had committed, that might help. So, I told her about the times I had been "naughty," and said, "Will God forgive me?"

She answered, "I'm sure He will if you promise not to do those things again."

This didn't give me a great deal of solace, so I asked her, "Well, every thing's just fine, isn't it?" She answered, "Yes, honey, now go back to bed."

My mother was ultra-religious. Sinfulness in our family was a no-no, and we were destined to go to Hell if we committed a sin. As I told my sister a few years ago, I think I failed childhood. It was just too much to deal with.

So, I was consoled by Mother but only temporarily. The thought didn't leave me, no matter how hard I tried to understand or forget it.

I tried to be active all the time as a means of averting my bad thoughts or falling into my habit of thinking the wrong way, but nothing helped. I would ride my bicycle the five blocks to see Ma, then would go to Mable's house, the mother of one of my fringe friends, Helen, who lived a couple of blocks away.

Mable was the neighborhood Mother Goose, a large, comfortable fat woman who listened to all the kids' problems and was properly sympathetic. We liked her because we felt safe with her. But I certainly couldn't tell Mable what was troubling me. For one thing, she wouldn't have understood. Nothing helped, not even Mable.

My school opening was drawing nearer, and the closer it loomed, the more apprehensive and worried I became. School openings always upset me and the stress at that time didn't help my mental state.

But perhaps in a distorted way it did. Apparently, I had reached the end of my rope. Having a fit and tearing up furniture, dishes—anything—was what I really wanted to do, but I had been taught not to be destructive, so I managed to squelch those urges.

One night, I was almost completely out of it.

I could function but couldn't communicate with anyone, so I went to the movies by myself.

The movie starred Peter Lorre and his then-wife, a young German actress named Karen Lorne who I thought was much too pretty for frog-eyed Peter.

While I was viewing the movie, the bad thought simply disappeared, and I knew I wasn't going to be bothered with it again. I didn't resolve my dilemma of not understanding it. It just went away. I guess my mind popped and, since I couldn't throw a fit and tear up something, the problem eased itself into the back of my consciousness.

I knew I would have to be extra careful never to say that phrase again (every thing is just fine), that if I even read it or heard someone else say it, it might come to the fore and trouble me again. From then on, that phrase became "The Five."

God in his goodness but oft mystical ways protects us from ourselves. When we can't stand something anymore, our mind heals itself. I've known this to happen several times since. Rarely have I given way to destructive fits, though I would have liked to. I never had an actual breakdown, but I think I had some "walking nervous breakdowns." As I stated before, I never directly missed a day's work or a day of school because of my mental state.

CHAPTER 18

SCHOOL STARTED, and the eighth grade got underway. Sylvia and Jeanie continued to torture me with their mind games and I still took it, my parents complaining in the background all the while.

We had a cute new boy at school, Georgie Rollins, who I flirted with in my own shy way, but to no avail. But the one nice boy who did pay attention to me, Jerry Williams, was too tall to suit me, so I rebuked him, foolishly. I think he asked me to a dance, but I wasn't ready for that yet.

To me, tall men's penises were about even with my head, and that was just too much to bear. I might have to see one. Worse still, I would have had to think of one. I didn't want that in my mind since it could cause thought trouble. I've never had this verified by any of my doctors, but I think that's the reason for my feeling the way I did at that time. I had no date with Jerry for that reason.

During this time Sylvia and Jeanie continued to be difficult. To further irritate them, I was invited to join a school-sponsored club, the Junior High Pep Club, which was a snobbish little sorority. There were 12 of us in the club, and we met at each other's homes for a business session and refreshments. Our purpose was to support athletic functions.

When I asked our sponsor, Miss Bradley, who was also our English teacher, and who probably suggested that I be taken in as a member, what was the purpose of the club, she said, "To go to the football games and yell for the local players."

In my klutzy way, I said, "But I don't like football," and I think Miss Bradley realized her first mistake with me. In addition to being inept in the social graces, I was also quite dumb. But I had made a good showing in her English classes. Also, we attended the same church, so she had taken me under her wing.

I plodded to football games, never really liking them and not understanding them. Yet, I managed to keep my head above water. I also felt like a fool when I tried to join the other club members in those ridiculous yells.

"Yea, team" would have sounded better to me if we had said "Yea, assholes," since none of the guys on the team even knew who I was and couldn't have cared less.

I decided to be good anyway and had no more "Crises," (as I called "The Five"), so life wasn't too traumatic. Not until Christmas.

Then my mother became quite ill with peritonitis and was hospitalized in Carterville, about 30 miles from Mooresville. Ma, who hadn't been living with us, came to help Daddy with Billie and me by getting us up in the morning, fixing meals, and just being there. My father went to Carterville every day to see Mother, sometimes taking Billie and me.

We weren't familiar with death and what it could mean, so weren't too concerned about Mother's condition even when Daddy told us, "I hate to tell you kids, but your mother might not pull through."

We were more concerned about Christmas, such as who would do the shopping for us, and take care of the usual amenities of Christmas Day gift-opening and dinner.

Mother came through the illness and was allowed to return home Christmas Day despite us being selfish little rascals. Ma, did her best at cooking the holiday dinner, and Christmas was good for us, and everyone managed to be civil.

When I returned to school after the Christmas break and saw Sylvia and Jeanie together for the first time, I asked them, "Did you know my mother was in the hospital?" Sylvia turned to Jeanie and said sarcastically, "See, I told you that would be the first thing she'd say."

For about the first time with these two clods, I felt my temper rising and stalked off. I was angry for a couple of days and, for once, they came to me. Not with apologies, of course, but with enough amenity that made it impossible for me not to be friendly. Anyway, I needed them, and they still needed someone to aggravate.

The rest of the year went by without too much trauma except for one particularly bad thing. I was good in math, but math scared me, and I was never on firm ground. We had a strong-willed teacher, Miss McCall, who was so cold she peed ice water.

We were into complex multiplication which I understood but didn't like because it made me nervous. I always did my homework correctly, and on one assignment we had about 20 problems to solve. I turned mine in, as I always did, but the next day, to my dismay, Miss McCall called me to her desk and asked why I hadn't turned in my homework for the previous day.

I told her, "I did turn it in," but she retorted, "Well, I don't have it and can't find it, so you'll have to do the problems again." This came as a shock since I was always a conscientious student.

I didn't tell my parents because perhaps they might have gone to Miss McCall, which would have upset me, so I did the problems over. But with this new problem added to the other dangers of being an eighth grader in a cruel world, I pondered on what I must do not to let this reoccur.

Then I decided I would have to do all my homework in duplicate. I also strived to do it with even more accuracy and, while I was afraid of making mistakes before this incident, I became petrified.

No one knew I meticulously copied all my math for my own reassurance, and after about a month of this, when no more papers were lost, I relaxed and stopped making copies.

CHAPTER 19

OTHER THAN THAT INCIDENT, life in the eighth grade wasn't so bad. There were no major "thought" traumas, though I was pretty much ensconced in my habit of worrying about every little fart. I still thought of my obsessions as a very bad habit, and one I prayed to God to overcome. I didn't think of it as an illness but a side effect of the fact that I didn't have much self-confidence. I still wasn't very popular, but I began branching out a little from Sylvia and Jeanie.

Roxanne was a young girl whose father also worked for the railroad and knew my father. Roxanne was an only child, and her doting over-protective parents had kept her at home the first seven grades of her schooling because they were afraid she would come in contact with germs.

Her mother was trained as a teacher, and so Roxanne was far ahead of the other eighth graders when finally, she was allowed to attend regular school. She was also a talented pianist, and though she had had very few piano lessons, could play anything once she heard it.

Roxanne lived in a middle-class neighborhood not far from our home, which was on the way to and from school. She and I began walking together, especially when it became obvious to me that Sylvia would rather have walked with Jeanie and left me to my own devices. Roxanne was a comfort because she was sweet, naïve and considerate. My parents approved of her also.

But Roxanne wasn't allowed out at night or on weekends and never went to the movies. I don't think she even went to church. There were germs there, also, you know.

Still, she invited me to her house often after school for hot chocolate or cake and milk. Her parents liked me, too, since they knew I wasn't going to lead their little flower astray. And I wasn't. Even with my deep, dark secrets concerning what I knew about sex, I wasn't going to tell anyone. They would have thought I was either evil or crazy, or both. I knew enough to keep that information to myself.

Roxanne and I became close and were friends for many years, although we took each other for granted. In our quest to attain a higher place on the social ladder, we didn't feel our relationship with each other was going to benefit our popularity. We both started out pretty much on the bottom rung, and our contact with each other only surfaced when there was a need for company.

Fortunately, we never quarreled, and now I wonder why I wasn't sadder when Roxanne died of leukemia at age 57. I don't think I ever gave her her due as a really true friend, one of the best I have ever had. Had I to do it over, I would in some way have told her how much I valued my relationship with her.

The only thing that exasperated me with Roxanne was her piano talent—she was either too shy or insecure to play the piano willingly. I almost always had to beg, "Please play the piano for me," often to no avail.

Perhaps Roxanne's mother's attitude had something to do with her reluctance to play. Anna would watch carefully while Roxanne played and would often, after only a few selections, go over and feel her forehead or under her arms for perspiration. If there was a trace of it, she'd say, "Roxanne, you're perspiring. You'd better stop playing the piano now."

I was amazed. Poor Roxanne. No wonder she had hang-ups, and that she had me, one of the rejects of society, as a best friend.

But sweet Roxanne served a purpose for me. She became a wedge between Sylvia and Jeanie and me, and I spent more and more time with her, but I still wanted to belong to Sylvia and Jeanie's club even though I was a member of the more prestigious pep club at school.

Soon I spent more and more time with Roxanne, though there was one more incident concerning Sylvia before I finally laid the debauchery to rest.

CHAPTER 20

When I began showing interest in joining the drum corps near the end of the eighth grade, my parents both felt the reason behind it was that Sylvia was also joining. That was part of the reason. Also, I just wanted to.

I had no musical talent or training, but I thought I could play a drum, and the corps was a pretty snappy group which performed at game half-times and in parades. So, I unwittingly got myself into another predicament.

But I didn't like our instructor, Mr. Humphrey.

Mr. Humphrey being large, surely had a big part in my dislike of him, but he also smelled funny like apple butter. While I liked apple butter, I didn't like it on him. He must have had it every morning for breakfast.

We started out learning to beat the drum. When he showed us the musical score, I didn't have the foggiest notion what he was talking about. So, I just tried to play along with the other girls and tap out the rhythms by rote, but I never did learn to play that thing.

I didn't understand formations, maneuvers or deployment either, and just couldn't get the whole marching strategy pictured in my mind. Unfortunately, I was on the front row and had no leader to follow; the other girls followed me.

I realized I was in way beyond my capabilities and wanted to drop out. However, my parents refused to let me quit. They said, "We know why you want to drop out. It's because Sylvia also gave up on it. You still want to do everything she does."

I tried to tell them, "No, that's not the reason. I just can't march and play that drum." But no matter what I said, they were adamant that I should continue in spite of Sylvia. I never could convince them that wasn't the real reason.

When school started, I was fitted in a kicky, pleated, cream-colored skirt and handsome militia-like jacket with a gold braid and buttons. But I still couldn't play the drum, though I had mastered some of the marching maneuvers. On the day of our first marching exhibition, the first home football game on the local field, I was the leader of my row of girls and was supposed to turn and retreat, with the other girls following me. But I missed my cue and turned to the right instead of to the left.

Since the entire school band was involved in this half-time procedure, the band major was responsible for seeing that all went well. He was close by when he saw me make the wrong turn, which would have really loused up the whole show. He took me by the shoulders and turned me to the left, but I could tell he was irritated.

I felt properly rebuked and embarrassed but somehow got through the half-time show. When I told my parents what had happened, they were concerned and contacted Mr. Humphrey.

Mr. Humphrey gently told them, "I think it best to let Jackie drop out of the corps." They had to agree, though reluctantly. So, ended my moment in the limelight.

Some children, and adults develop learning blocks in different subjects, and I think that's what afflicted me in the drum corps. If it couldn't be written down in black and white, or if I couldn't see a picture of whatever was being described, I couldn't comprehend it. Consequently, I couldn't figure it out.

CHAPTER 21

THE NINTH GRADE LOOMED, and I had no serious mental problems that fall. And to distract me from any problems I might have had was a handsome young man.

His name was Carlo Pettinaro and he, his mother, father and brother, Roberto, who was a year younger, had moved from Michigan to Mooresville where his father had purchased the local bakery.

Carlo had black, straight, neat hair, dancing black eyes and a killer smile with dimples and nice teeth. In addition to all that, he was also unbelievably nice. All the girls went wild over him. Roberto, who was Billie's age, was not as handsome but was attractive in his own way. He had auburn hair, hazel eyes, and a few freckles. Right away Billie and I staked them out as ours. But such was not to be.

As fall went on, I was as friendly and as nice to Carlo as I knew how to be. He was very nice to me; unfortunately, he was nice to everyone.

Then came the event of the Sadie Hawkins Barn Dance

where girls could ask boys to go if they wanted to. I desperately longed to ask Carlo but knew if he didn't want to go and refused me, I would be devastated.

I wanted Billie to ask Roberto, and she said, "I will if you'll ask Carlo." But I just couldn't get up the nerve to do so. One Saturday, I talked her into going down to the bakery where the boys were working telling them that she and I wanted to take both of them.

While Billie was on her mission of the heart, I was at home nervously wringing my hands and hoping against hope they'd go with us. But, when Billie returned, she gave some vague reason why they couldn't go, saying, "We might as well forget them. I think they have girlfriends."

Later Billie admitted that she couldn't ask them, and I certainly don't blame her. I should have gone with her. Instead, I went to the dance alone and hung out with the other wallflowers, but Billie asked her close friend, Bob Wallace, and he gladly went.

Billie was much more outgoing than I. She wasn't as shy as I was and was a very pretty brunette. She had no trouble getting boys to notice her and was coming along nicely within the realm of social graces. The same could not be said of me.

At the dance, where we, fortunately, wore cotton pinafores or something similarly casual, we were doing a fast snake dance when I fell flat on my chin. I received a deep cut about three-quarters of an inch wide along the chin bone.

Of course, I bled all over everything causing the chaperones to call my parents and get me to the doctor. Our family doctor, Dr. Wilson, was of the old school where doctors felt it was part of their oath to accommodate patients, so he met us at his office.

I was quite frightened that I would have to have stitches since I knew it would be painful, but he said, "No, you won't. I think we can just press that cut flesh in so there will be a neat scar with no puffiness." Fortunately, it turned out that way; the scar scarcely shows.

I attracted a lot of attention and was allowed to wear my chin bandaged for a couple of weeks. And I glowed in the attention I received. Kids are so pathetic—it only takes a busted chin to make them happy.

Before I move on, it should be noted that Sylvia and Jeanie's friendship had also fallen by the wayside. Always a pretty, delicate, little blonde with big blue eyes, Jeanie had become even prettier. She had a reputation as the beauty of the class.

She won all the beauty contests, and much to the aggravation of the other budding girls her age began winning the hearts of all the cute young males.

While I couldn't stand Jeanie (even when I was posing as her friend), I disliked her, even more, when it became apparent that Carlo had finally lost his heart to her!

I just couldn't believe why any self-respecting young man, who could have had anyone he wanted, would pick such an unscrupulous girl.

But Carlo was still my friend, though I realized I had to look elsewhere for a boyfriend.

CHAPTER 22

While I wasn't really looking, the love bug bit me in the form of Donnie Ellers, also, a ninth grader who attended the same church we did.

Donnie was also a member of my Sunday School class and Sunday evening Christian Endeavor group. That's when serious flirting took place; we were more informal and playful than ordinarily one would be at church, and Donnie, who was quite handsome, began feeling his oats and coming out of his shell.

I was shy, also, but had learned how to give meaningful glances and inquire a little about his large family. Donnie's closest brother was Georgie, who, like Roberto and Carlo, was a year younger than Donnie—Billie's age. Billie liked Georgie, so we replaced the Pettinaro brothers with the Ellers brothers in our pursuit of boys.

The romance with Donnie budded during the holiday season. We went caroling one Sunday night, and Donnie surreptitiously slipped his hand around mine, and I didn't object. In fact, I liked it. Our minister, Rev. Cobb, was walking with us and observed what was going on. He apparently approved of the match.

The local movie theatre was our favorite place to spend Saturday afternoon. Those corny Old Western movies were only a backdrop for hand-holding, nuzzling, and getting acquainted.

Donnie asked me one Friday at school, "Can I take you to the show tomorrow afternoon?"

A real date! That was a first for me, and I anxiously looked forward to it. But I was also worried. I asked Mother, "Do you think Donnie will pay my way into the show?"

She answered, "He surely will, or he wouldn't have asked you to go with him."

To save myself any embarrassment, I urged her to give me a quarter to tie in the corner of a handkerchief. In case he didn't pay my admission, I wouldn't be left standing on the sidewalk. I was so insistent, she gave me the quarter.

Donnie walked all the way across town to pick me up, then back six blocks to the theatre. When we arrived at the box office, Donnie went straight to the box office to get what I hoped were two tickets. But I managed to stand as close as I could to the cashier's cage, so I could hear whether or not he purchased two tickets.

He did, and I was very relieved. By now, you must know that I was very insecure and did everything the hard way. But I enjoyed the afternoon and saved my quarter. I didn't even have to buy popcorn—Donnie bought that.

I was elated with Donnie. Here was my first boyfriend and one my parents approved of—primarily because he went to our church. While his parents didn't attend, they seemed to be upright citizens, respectable, middle-class and sober.

While I was busy trying to divest myself of Sylvia and Jeanie—Jeanie had long since gone into the affections of Carlo, bringing all kinds of plaudits and popularity for her because of that coup—the Lawsons moved into our neighborhood.

The presence of Bobby Lawson didn't bother me anymore (I think I had loosened up in my attitude toward the male species because of Donnie) and Billie and I had another friend in Betty Lawson, who was Billie's age.

The Lawsons were an unusual breed. They just rented houses all over town during the time I knew them.

The house they moved into a block away from us was quite nice for a rental home. Added to the advantage, was that Jodie had a car and drove Betty and Bobby to school. So, Billie and I managed to ride with them often, especially if it was a rainy day.

This was war-time, and with all the aggravations of getting gasoline and tires for our auto, my dad had decided to sell our car. In rainy weather, we depended upon our umbrellas and raingear.

One day in the spring of that year, Jodie picked us up during a heavy rain. Betty sat in the front seat with her mother.

Since it was report card day, Jodie asked, "How did you two girls do on your grade cards?"

Billie and I related that we had all A's. She then asked, "Betty, how did you do?"

Betty truthfully told her mother, "I got B's and C's."

With that answer, Jodie hauled off and backhanded her with her right hand, smack in the face.

Jodie had always been competitive with my parents about their offspring and apparently just couldn't handle this latest defeat in Betty, so she bopped her. Of course, Betty cried, and Billie and I were embarrassed and uncomfortable. We felt a great deal of sympathy for Betty, whom we liked and felt the slap was unpardonable.

While we didn't always think we had good parents, we knew they would never have slapped us in front of other people, or even in private. After that, we steered as clear of Jodie as possible, realizing she had a very mean streak.

But Jodie got to me later, good grades or not, which I'll relate in a bit. I have additional dumb stories to share with you before I get to her revenge.

CHAPTER 23

NOT LONG AFTER the incident in Jodie's car, I brought disgrace upon myself having to do with my hair. It was curly and pretty or, at least, all of my life people had been telling me so.

Since I was on the staff of our junior high newspaper, which was published twice a month, I was always thinking up subjects to write about that would be both interesting and amusing. What I thought up in the period after the holidays now embarrasses me, and I wonder how I could have been so brazen and untoward.

Often the school newspaper staffs would concoct the "perfect" girl or boy, assembling all the best characteristics of the subjects into one super being, i.e., "so-and-so's hair, teeth, legs, mouth, etc." I suggested that we have the junior high version of both sexes and without the slightest blink of an eye, said we could let the girl have my hair.

I don't know what the others on the staff thought or said about me, but I can well imagine. Anyway, they did as I had suggested but it was something I didn't want mentioned in my presence. I just chose to ignore it once it was finished.

Then a funny thing happened. I began pulling my hair out in about an inch-square area over my forehead. I couldn't help myself but, fortunately, I could comb the remaining front hair over the spot, and I don't think anyone ever noticed it. That's what psychiatrists now call Trichotillomania, I understand.

At the same time, I didn't wash my hair for at least six weeks. It was as though I was punishing myself for my ill-advised action in the school newspaper article. Some of the other girls, said, "Boy Jackie, your hair certainly needs washing. It's not even curly." Mother finally ordered me to wash it.

It's a bit mystifying but, during all this, that Donnie didn't seem to notice my hair problems, or because of shyness, he didn't mention them. Of course, we weren't into heavy petting—just hand-holding and an occasional kiss—so perhaps it evaded him.

After I washed my hair, my fascination with pulling it out diminished and I returned to as normal as I could be at that time. But a traumatic incident occurred that had all of the students in both junior and senior high in a trauma. Carlo died.

That Carlo was a very popular student is an understatement. He was liked our "star" in residence. While I had long-shelved any romantic notion toward him, he was still my friend. Then, one day in his phys ed class, the boys were running ordinary relays in the gymnasium. He slipped and fell at the end of a race, ramming his head against the concrete block wall. He was immediately knocked out and never did regain consciousness. He died that night at home of excessive bleeding in the brain.

School authorities, or anyone who works with young people, have since learned that a loss of that type deals quite a blow to the other youngsters, especially if he's someone as well thought of as Carlo. Now, after a major disaster, the students are often counseled. But in Mooresville in 1943, there were no counselors or therapists, so we had to handle our grief in our own way.

I was very sad and wrote poetry about Carlo. I never let anyone see it and, later, during a spell of guilt, I burned my diary, so it was lost forever.

Most teenagers welcome the excuse to sink into a melancholy state, and all of us were very bereft during that period. But in all due tribute to Carlo and to his grieving family, it was a very sad occurrence and just cause for grieving.

I'm sure it required a long time, if perhaps forever, for Carlo's family to accept what had happened to their lovely son, and none of us were really surprised when, at the end of the school year, they sold their bakery back to the former owners and returned to Michigan. They couldn't tolerate Mooresville or their memories any longer.

They kept in touch with some of their friends in town, Roberto with his buddies and Jeanie. We later learned Roberto went into the navy, finished college, and became a multi-millionaire through laundry products he developed.

But Carlo's death lingered on for many of us, especially at Mooresville High School. I think those emotionally defective, such as I, like to be sad and will nurse a situation as long as possible. Also, in all fairness to me, adolescents have a difficult time with their sorrow and tend to be considerably more emotional than more mature persons are. Carlo was on our minds for a long, long time.

Adding to the poignancy of our memories was Victor Herbert's haunting song, "Lover, Come Back to Me," which the senior high choir presented in its spring concert held quite close after Carlo's death. That accented our grief and was the topic of my poem in his remembrance. As unpoetic as I've always been, I'm curious to know what I wrote in that poem. But once I wrote it, I didn't look at it again.

Alas, as we all know, love unnourished soon dies, so mine in the real world did also. I still had Donnie, but he was becoming a bit tiresome. However, the attention he had received through his alliance with me (that he was dateable and romantic fodder) helped his ego a great deal. I suspect now but didn't at the time that he was finding me a bit tiresome, too.

Then apparently, it was time for Mother to leave again. She hadn't left in quite a while, maybe a year or two, but in April of that year, she and my father got into another row, and I had what must have been my first display of a violent reaction.

All of a sudden, with my parents arguing and Billie and me as bystanders, I collapsed onto the floor on my hands and knees and pounded the floorboards screaming, "I just can't stand any more of this. Will you two SHUT UP?"

I surprised all of them, and poor Billie reacted with a nervous laugh. She said, "Why is she doing that? What's wrong with her?" She tried to pull me up, all the while laughing hysterically, and my dad came over to pick me up also, admonishing me for acting in that manner.

My parents were annoyed with me, but it did interrupt their argument for a while. I cried a good bit, but, then realizing I could do nothing more, composed myself and tried to go on. With an inner strength that surprises me, I sloughed off the incident.

But this didn't deter Mother from leaving as she had threatened during their argument, so off she went, probably to her parents' home.

When she left it upset me a great deal; I became very apprehensive all the time she was gone. My ability to compose myself never did come to the fore. I was greatly upset and wondered what our future held. Who was going to get us up for school and who was going to cook for us, and wash and iron our clothes? *Would she ever come back*? I wondered. I was embarrassed and didn't want the neighbors or any of my friends to know she was gone.

When we were with the other young people in the neighborhood, such as Betty and Bobby Lawson, I didn't want them to know and especially I did not want their mother, Jodie, to know. I didn't trust her or like her and knew she would delight in our unhappiness and discomfiture.

Mother wasn't gone too long that time; Daddy went to get her after she had been away two nights. He was disgusted and told her, "You have no business running off like that with two growing daughters to care for. It's a very foolish thing to do."

Usually, Mother wouldn't return home until my dad promised she could have her way, but this time, his indignation prevailed. That was her last elopement and attempt at independence.

CHAPTER 24

NINTH GRADE GRADUATION LOOMED, and that was the beginning of the end for Donnie and me. Being very unsure of myself, I naturally wanted to be just like the other girls and not stand out in any way. But such was not to be.

One of my mother's friends, Abigail Burris, had a magnificent garden which was in full bloom in May of that year and she told Mother she wanted to make my corsage. MAKE a corsage? How could they expect me to wear a homemade job when all the other girls would have professionally arranged flowers? But they did, and I did, though very unhappily and with lots of excuses.

To add to the difficulty of the situation, a number of the graduates were invited to a post-graduation party at Anna Jo Caldwell's home, Donnie and I among them. Anna Jo was the offspring of an old, wealthy family, and to be invited was considered quite a coup.

Then I realized Donnie didn't have a suit and wouldn't be wearing one even at the graduation ceremony but would wear a cardigan sweater instead. That was his usual church wear, and somehow, I found out that his parents couldn't afford to buy him a suit.

We went to the party, me with my homemade corsage and Donnie in his sweater. I felt miserable; as if everyone was looking at us. The two of us sat in a corner, and I couldn't wait to get out of there. I'm sure it didn't go unnoticed by Anna Jo and the other girls that perhaps I wasn't quite polished enough at that time to handle a bad situation. Unsurprisingly, I wasn't invited to any more parties for a while.

Donnie, of course, sensed I wasn't pleased with him. Consequently, our relationship became edgy and uncomfortable. He wasn't so enamored of me as he had once been, nor I of him.

I let him down gently. He wasn't quite so kind to me. He dumped me for Betty Lawson.

To make matters worse, Jodie, the Witch of the East End, gloatingly told me the day of their first date, "Well, Betty took your boyfriend away from you, didn't she? Maybe she won't come up to your grades, but she does better than you when it comes to boys."

I was flabbergasted that she would talk to me in such a way, and I tried in vain to tell her I was tired of Donnie. I said, "I was getting tired of him anyway, so it really doesn't matter to me." But Jodie, in her arrogant way, just scoffed and didn't believe me.

She reveled in her daughter's victory, and I steered clear of her after that. She was too much for me, just a 15-year-old. I didn't tell my mother, as usual, and had I done so, I'm quite sure she would have flailed Jodie verbally.

CHAPTER 25

AFTER THE BIG DONNIE ROMANCE, I didn't have a steady boyfriend right away but went to the movies with some of the boys from church in whom I wasn't particularly interested. No, I had a new range of interest: older men!

And how did I come in contact with these older men of at least 31 or 32 years of age? Babysitting! I was the Deluxe Babysitter, the model for all adolescent girls to follow had they wanted to make a good impression as a little mother, confidante, and housekeeper all for just 50 cents an evening! Those people really screwed me, and it makes me angry now that they took advantage of one so young.

But I was in my glory. I loved the little kids and the knowledge that I was needed and important. For just 50 cents, I washed up the supper dishes, bathed the kids, read to them, and got them in bed. I gave up all semblance of a social life to be available when my growing list of appreciative customers needed me. After all, *I was a bargain so why shouldn't they be nice to me?*

In addition to the kids, I began liking the husbands...too much. Having never considered myself a femme fatale or having much charm, I had somehow learned to flirt outrageously. At 15, I had gone from a straight-figured little girl to one with a few curves.

Unfortunately for me, I was also seductive, and those fathers thought I could be more than a babysitter. Some of the wives got suspicious, too, but since I came at such a good rate, they didn't want to give me up and so tolerated a few meaningful looks and outright flirting on my part.

But I didn't score with any of the men, at least not then. They were attentive to me and reciprocated with the usual male chauvinism engendered toward a young, inexperienced girl. However, they all knew I was jail-bait, so they left me alone. Physically, that is. Some of them were probably going through their mid-life crisis and attention from a young girl no doubt was a titillating boost for their fading egos.

Then, too, this was World War II, and none of these men were in the military, for whatever reason. The attitude of men in those days was either to serve their country or be considered a piker. No doubt there were several bruised egos cruising around.

I thought all that flirting was innocent since I knew, deep down, I would NEVER consider sex with any of them, and I wouldn't have sex until I was married. That was my dictum, and, in my mind, seduction wasn't necessarily a sin as long as it didn't include sex. I had by then loosened up my rigid attitude toward men in general, and sex in particular. But being a virgin was still of the utmost importance to me.

While all this innocent flirting didn't go past an occasional hand-clasp, I didn't limit showering my charms on just the fathers of my babysitting wards. There were other handsome men in the community who I thought would benefit from my scintillating charms. I found that a smile and come-hither glance went a long way toward attracting attention, although I continued to consider it harmless. But then I met my Waterloo.

CHAPTER 26

YOU MAY WONDER what had happened to the "Habit" that plagued me in earlier years, resulting in the "thought trouble" I suffered. It was still there in the form of making foolish decisions and being unsure of myself.

However, this new attention was good for my ego, too, and helped allay some of the symptoms of whatever was wrong with my mind. I was by far not the confident young girl I would liked to have been, and since the boys at school completely ignored me, I was happy to be appreciated by the parents—men in particular. Like I said, I eventually met more than I could handle.

Waterloo came in two phases: First, there was Tom. I met him through my older cousin, Mary, with whom I was quite close to after Ma died. She was a grown-up young woman by then. Her alcoholic, abused husband, Otto, had left and she was on her own. I suspect Otto finally got enough of Mary's beatings after his frequent bouts of drunkenness.

Mary, who had little formal education, worked at the

local laundry and, because she was a big, strong girl, and there was a shortage of employable males in that wartime era, she was promoted to drive the laundry delivery van. She liked the job, and it paid better than actual work in the laundry.

Mary's run extended to nearby Camp Crippen and, since she was tall, slim, and pretty with dimples, she attracted a lot of beaus. One was Ray, who came from the Chicago area, and he was nice company until his monthly payday when he always managed to have a good overnight drunk.

Mary should have known better from her experience with Otto, but, as we've all learned, mistakes often do not breed wisdom. I think she got drunk with him, but she didn't beat him up the way she did Otto. He, in turn, didn't aggravate her by disappearing for several days with frequent liaisons with other women. He was just a true-blue drunk, and Mary liked him.

Naturally, Ray had buddies who accompanied him to Mooresville on his visits to Mary, and often Billie, and I would meet these "soldiers," as my dad referred to them. When my dad found out the servicemen were around his two daughters, he threw a fit.

He firmly forbade us against being in their company and told us, "If I ever catch you when any of those soldiers show up at Mary's, there's going to be real trouble. I want you to immediately come home, and don't lie to me because I'll find out."

We knew he would, too. In Daddy's mind, servicemen were no good, love-them-and-leave-them rascals. Perhaps he was right. He didn't consider his allegiance to his country to include letting those young men dally with his two daughters. Camp Crippen and anyone service-connected were off limits to us. We didn't like that, but we knew our father well enough not to cross him.

CHAPTER 27

MARY HAD OTHER CONTACTS Daddy didn't know about and, had he known, they would have been verboten for his daughters. I'm referring to Mary's employer, J. R. Clinton, and his lascivious son, Tom.

During that summer of '43, after my romance with Donnie had fizzled, I spent quite a bit of time with Mary, who mainly wanted to teach me to drive. Rather, I wanted to learn and hounded her until she taught me the rudiments of driving the floor-stick laundry van.

I was a terrible driver with no sense of coordination. When I got behind the wheel, there was no telling where the vehicle might go. Mary was smart enough to pick quiet, traffic-less streets for me to practice on, but I never did master the trick of releasing the clutch at the same time as I maneuvered the floor gear-shift lever. I didn't wreck the van but played havoc with its inner apparatus.

Then Tom, who worked at menial jobs at the laundry during that summer vacation, asked me one day, "Would you like to go to the movies with me?"

Of course, being dateless at the time, I said, "Yes." Tom was two years older than me and would be a senior at high school in the fall. Daddy thought that was too old, but I insisted he was a nice boy and well thought of.

Tom wasn't nearly as handsome as his father and had funny teeth. Of course, the Clintons, who had plenty of money, hadn't spared the expense on Tom's teeth and he had been undergoing treatment, with braces and all kinds of apparatuses for several years. But nothing seemed to help his teeth and, I think, when he became of age, he just had them all removed for false ones.

Anyway, Tom was popular in school, having been elected president of the student body for his senior year. Daddy let me go out with him but, sadly, he measured up to his expectations. The minute we returned home from the movies, he was busy with his hands.

I asked him, "Would you like to sit down on the yard lawn swing?" He readily agreed because it was farther away from the house than the front porch—and Daddy.

I hardly had time to collect myself when his hand sped up my skirt to where it shouldn't have gone. I immediately protested, and he stopped, but after a few kisses, which I didn't enjoy he was back with the hands. So, finally, I told him, "I have to go in now," and he left probably with a bruised ego, but I didn't care.

The next day at dinner, when we usually had our family discussions, Daddy asked me, "How did you enjoy the movies with 'Squirrely?'" Of course, he was referring to Tom.

I had to admit to myself that Tom did have teeth like a squirrel, but, being very sensitive to criticism, my father's remark hurt my feelings. I liked Tom, except for his hand-work, and hoped he would come back, and I didn't like my father referring to my boyfriend that way.

I managed to utter, "All right, but I wish you wouldn't call him that." Still, the name stuck with my father for as long as Tom came around.

Tom did come back, but his manners hadn't improved, so finally I tired of him. This was about the same time my father (probably having heard that Tom was a fast opera-tor), decided I couldn't go out with him, anyway, and told me to break it off. I didn't really mind too much.

And then there was J.R. I spent quite a bit of time with Mary that summer, and I wasn't above giving J. R. a few glances when I accompanied Mary to the laundry.

One Saturday afternoon when Mary and I were there (she worked on Saturdays although the machine workers only worked Saturday morning), J.R. sent Mary out to buy some ice cream for us.

The minute she left, J.R. called me back into the laun-dry workroom. I surely knew what he intended to do, but I was naïve, having never gone past the looking stage and hand-holding. I was quite surprised when he planted a very mature kiss on me. But I liked it, although in my mind it was wrong because he was married.

Mary knew what had gone on and, when she drove me home, she told me not to come back to the laundry, or she would be forced to tell Daddy. But she didn't tell me not to go visit her in her convenient apartment in the basement of his home. I only ventured over there once and, when J.R. learned I was there, he immediately came down since he lived close by. Mary, being no fool and not wanting to upset my dad, sent me home pronto.

She saw how I looked at J.R., and deduced, correctly, that I desired more of the brief morsel of passion I had experienced at the laundry. In no uncertain terms, she also told me not to come back to the apartment, thus ending my first sinful experience with the older men with whom I was so enamored. Unfortunately, Mary couldn't be around all the time to rescue me from similar situations. But, bless her, she tried.

Thus, ended my experiences with J.R. and Tom, thanks to Mary and Daddy. I didn't miss Tom, and I soon stopped remembering J.R.'s very sensual kiss. I later realized I was fortunate not to have gotten mixed up with him, but I still flirted with him whenever I saw him. Of father and son, I'd rate J.R. as a 10 and Tom as a possibly good three. Tom didn't have the finesse his father had by far.

CHAPTER 28

THEN I HAD another CRISIS, a "thought-trouble" crisis. This time it was over the word "Suspend."

Probably because of my imagined dalliances and actual seductiveness toward those men, which I knew to be bad as ingrained into me through my religious upbringing and strong moral training, I suffered with more worrisome thoughts. As some of my doctors said later, the thought problems, which they termed "symptoms," were often generated by feelings of guilt. I've noticed that, during periods of stress, or especially when I knew I was doing something wrong, my Habit came to the fore.

That summer of 1943, after I settled down from the Clinton escapades, I began to worry again. I reverted to being unable to read and comprehend what I had read and had very little self-confidence. I felt as though everything I did was wrong.

I didn't get back to "The Five" because I knew I couldn't say the phrase without getting into trouble, but to alleviate the worries that plagued me, I decided to put them on "suspension." In other words, I wouldn't fret about those worries that popped up frequently, but I would suspend them until I felt better and could think about them more clearly.

But eventually, that didn't work, and I became obsessed with the word "suspend." I tried to picture the meaning of the word in my mind but merely contorted it. It was another bugaboo, although not as serious as the one that had tortured me two years earlier. Naturally, I couldn't talk about what I was struggling with to anyone; they either would have thought I was crazy or wouldn't have understood what I was saying.

So, for most of August, before school began, I was engrossed by this thought, and mad as a hatter. The beginning of school probably added stress, and, as my doctors later told me, it most likely worsened my condition.

CHAPTER 29

WHEN SCHOOL GOT UNDERWAY, with new clothes, new students, and two attractive new female teachers, my attention diverted from thinking "suspend" over and over again and trying to get everything right. Eventually, the obsession disappeared without ever having been resolved. It was then added to the collection of those words and images I couldn't think about, relegated to the murkiness of my mind.

I wasn't quite so affable toward the male species after the Clintons; in fact, I became downright reclusive and had no dates at all. My demeanor was serious, and I went from a playful flirt to a grouchy teenager.

But I did develop a new interest—pen pals! Letters and names of young people from throughout the country wanting pen pals appeared in our church newsletter. I only wrote to the girls, and I soon had a contingent of friends-through-the-mail from coast to coast.

We exchanged pictures and facts about ourselves and

families, and I eagerly went home from school each day to see what I had in the mail.

Then came the bad part. Since my life was so mundane, except for my fantasies about the older men who I thought were attractive, I distorted the facts. Or, in plain English, I fabricated a whole new personality for myself about how out-going I was, how many boyfriends I had, and facts about my exciting social life. I thought this was all harmless fun, but I soon began to live through those letters. They were my main interest in life, although I didn't allow my studies to go undone.

The trouble was, I wrote so many lies that I had to write them all down, so I could keep an account of them and not contradict myself. I was living in a dream world.

Daddy took note of the letters. He didn't read them or my notebook containing the fibs I had told. He just felt I was spending too much time writing them, and not taking part in the everyday world around me as a normal teenager. He questioned the advisability of writing all those letters, and I became upset by what I considered to be criticism and interference.

I was very angry with him and thought to myself—and sometimes out loud to him: "He doesn't want me to have any friends, just like he always did. He never has liked any of my friends."

Part of this was true. My parents were very particular when it came to our friends. They didn't think Billie and I chose them wisely, and that they were a bad influence. I understand their caution now, but at that time, I was suspicious of their motives concerning my letter-writing. One time, when I hadn't received any letters for a couple of days, I accused Daddy of hiding them from me.

He was indignant and said, "Why would I hide them from you? You should know better than that, although I don't think it's healthy for you to write so many."

This vicarious activity continued for most of that school year and into the next, but my mail pals began to tire of the venture, I suspect, as I did also, and the letters dwindled. Truth be known, their outpourings to me were probably almost as fabricated as mine. Who's to know? I never met any of them, and they did not continue into my adulthood. But it was fun for a while, though not necessarily healthy.

Soon, a new year beckoned, and the winds of change were in the air.

CHAPTER 30

THE WORD SPREAD AROUND town that Billie and I were among the best babysitters from the standpoint of responsibility, dependability, and wholesomeness. The parents trusted us with their children; they also had heard that most of the children liked us. So, we were getting into the upper echelon of babysitting and sitting for some pronounced members of society.

One fateful day Barbara Gebhart called and wanted us to babysit early the next morning while she attended a brunch. We had heard of the Gebharts. Richard Gebhart was the publisher of the local daily newspaper. He was a new businessman in town, and we knew the couple was in their mid-30s. They also had two children, Dickie, four years old, and Janie, about nine months.

Billie and I were delighted to be called by this upper crust family. We readily accepted and said we would be over on time, so Barbara could get to her party. We walked all the way across the town to where the Gebharts lived in a nice rented house.

When we arrived, Barbara had left for her brunch, and Richard was struggling with the children, trying to get little Dickie to eat and taking care of Janie, who had a smelly diaper.

Right away, Billie and I took over. We told little Dickie, "Now, eat, or we'll just take your cereal away from you." With this no-nonsense approach, Dickie ate.

Then we tended to little Janie, a beautiful, sweet little baby. The senior Gebhart knew we were in control, so he left for his office. We straightened up the house, washed up the breakfast dishes, and entertained the kids. The household was buzzing right along when Barbara returned from her brunch.

This made quite an impression on the Gebharts. They knew we could create calm out of havoc.

Then when Barbara realized we had walked all the way across town, rather than having been transported by car, she told us, "I'll take you home and, in the future, if you sit with us, either Richard or I will pick you up. It's ridiculous for you to walk."

And so, began a long-time friendship between our family and the Gebharts, one that boded good and bad.

Barbara was a nice, cultured, educated young woman and very kind to Billie and me. She was also quite pretty, but both of us were struck with Richard's handsomeness and vitality, and secretly felt Barbara wasn't pretty enough for him. He was young—only 34 when we met him—and had already brought the local newspaper up to new excellence and profit.

Our first inkling of him had come earlier when he played piano with some other businessmen in the town who presented a jazz medley at our high school one day during assembly. It wasn't lost on most of the girls in the crowd that Richard was good-looking, dashing, and a talented musician.

Richard also liked to flirt. So, I added him to my list of the older men I admired. First off, I liked both Richard and Barbara, and they seemed to appreciate Billie and me for our sense of responsibility and general intelligence. I liked the children, too. They were cute, well-behaved little kids, except once in a while when Dickie lost his temper. I later discovered he was quite insecure and became easily upset, especially if he had to wait on either of his parents to arrive to pick him up.

Financially, my paltry salary of 50 cents a night didn't change, and I still did the dinner dishes and took care of all the loose ends. Billie decided she didn't want to babysit as much as I did in the early summer because she had a steady boyfriend.

That made me the chief babysitter and dishwasher. But the Gebharts seemed so appreciative of me that I felt elated; successful, too, since I had always thought I was pretty dumb and didn't do much of anything right.

My poor morale was boosted when, early in the fall of that year, Barbara told me, "We want to go to Knoxville for the weekend to visit Richard's mother, but don't want to take the kids. Do you think you could stay with them?"

The fact that they trusted me enough to be left alone with the kids the entire weekend greatly added to my self-esteem. Although I couldn't drive, nor did I have a driver's license or access to a car, there were no problems since I didn't have to get out for anything all weekend.

Barbara planned the meals and left messages for where to reach them in Knoxville. They were also going to a newspaper conference. I felt like Little Miss Housemother and relished the independence and responsibility I was given.

At that time a romantic interest in Richard didn't exist; I plainly thought both Barbara and Richard were the greatest people I had ever met. And they made an effort to become friendly with my parents and to let them know how much they trusted and needed me.

The weekend went very well with no problems. On Sunday I took the children for a long walk. I remember putting on my only suit, a pin-check in beige, light blue, and white that my mother had made for me. I don't think I had had a nicer day in my entire life than that day. I was absolutely euphoric.

I thought, "This is the grandest thing that has ever happened to me. These people have put a lot of trust in me." I realized I was only 16 years old and it was a big responsibility.

Then the symptoms returned. But this time they weren't triggered by problems but by a positive advent.

I had just begun my junior year in high school and had enrolled for typing and beginning shorthand. One night, as Richard was taking me home, he asked, "What are you studying in school?"

I told him about the commercial courses I was taking, and he said, "If you do well and learn to type and take shorthand, I'll give you a job at the newspaper next summer."

Imagine! A job at the newspaper! *Wow, was that incredible news!*

I told my parents right away, and they thought that was fine. But then my thought trouble began. I wondered: *Had I really heard him correctly? Did he mean that or was it just an empty promise he'd give to a young girl? And what kind of work would I be doing, and could I do it?*

I went over and over in my mind exactly what he had said about the job because it was so important to me. This was another symptom of my "Habit," going over and over whatever troubled me.

So, I studied diligently and became the best student in shorthand, but typing was another matter. Perhaps my coordination wasn't any better than it had been when I was in that nerdy drum corps, but I just couldn't type. My difficulties were probably also due to nervousness since I wanted so much to succeed.

Finally, I told my parents, "I need a typewriter at home to practice on, and since I've saved some of my babysitting money, I can pay half for a used one." We knew we couldn't get a new one; this was war-time.

The machine we found at an office supply store was an old Underwood circa 1920s, but in good condition and it worked well. My parents also purchased a typing manual to help me learn at home, which I did, and I actually became quite adept once I had established a little confidence.

CHAPTER 31

BEFORE LONG and for whatever reason, Mother had had photos taken of Billie and me, probably by a traveling photographer.

When I mentioned this to Barbara, she said. "We'd like to have a copy of one of the small ones to put on our mantle." That pleased me.

Not long afterward it was try-out time for the junior class play which, that year, was another comedy geared for high schools called "Brother Goose."

I told the Gebharts I was going to audition. Richard said, "I know the drama teacher and director of the play, and I'll put in a good word for you." Well, a "good word" from Richard meant a dictum to be followed, or else. Richard had a lot of influence in the community and used it.

Sure enough, Mr. Smith gave me the second female lead, Lenore, the unpleasant society fiancée of the leading man.

Then, too, was the matter of costumes. Of course, Lenore would have been well-dressed, so Barbara, out of kindness, offered to loan me some of her clothing since we were about the same size.

She had a beautiful brown gabardine suit which was very popular at the time and also owned a purple wool suit with a gold buckle adorning the left front. She also loaned me some of her beautiful, expensive, high-heel sling pumps, which were the mode of the day, as we also had the same foot size. There were other garments, too, and I thought it was very kind of Barbara to loan me her expensive garb.

Shortly before the play was to be presented, I was scheduled to babysit with the Gebhart children. When I arrived at the house, Richard playfully suggested. "Look around the living room for something different. We have a surprise for you."

I couldn't imagine what he was talking about and saw nothing out of place or new. When I told Richard and Barbara, on their return from their evening out, that I didn't find anything unusual, Richard said, "Just wait. You'll see."

The next day the surprise was unveiled. My picture was in the paper along with the other two leads in the play, proclaiming the upcoming event. I was pleasantly surprised since my photo had never appeared in the newspaper before and wasn't likely to be in the future unless I committed some heinous crime.

I realized the item missing from their living room was my picture which had been on the mantle. It had been taken to the office for a "cut" to be made

But I was awful in that play, and I think my friends and relatives agreed with me. They told me I was good with an embarrassed tone in their voices, but I knew I wasn't. I forgot where the poison ivy prop was placed, muffed my lines, and was generally scared to death.

I wish I had been mature enough to tell Richard not to do me any more favors. That event is something I don't like to think about. I didn't try out for the senior class play because I was as poor an actress as I was a drum corps performer. Perhaps this explains why my success as a babysitter and the fact that these nice people appreciated me so much, made such an impression upon me. I wasn't accustomed to being a winner.

CHAPTER 32

IN MARCH, the month of my birthday, the Gebharts thought it would be nice to treat to treat my mother and me (her birthday was the day after mine) to a concert in nearby Springfield. We would hear the famous String Quartet, a group of ever-changing musicians which had been well-known for several decades.

Mother even went out and bought a new suit. I had finally acquired a gabardine suit, so we were all suited up for the occasion. But in addition to my lack of self-confidence and social graces, I was worried about Mother because I knew she had even less social than I was.

I'm ashamed to say, she embarrassed me, but I'm sure the Gebharts found her to be charming. I was so sensitive to what I thought was my mother's shortcomings that I was uncomfortable but too young to know I needn't have been.

Right away Mother told Barbara and Richard: "This is practically my first store-bought suit; I always make my clothes as well as those of my daughters."

That embarrassed me, but I'm sure it delighted the Gebharts to see how enthusiastic she was about their invitation, and that she was thoroughly enjoying herself.

My mom enjoyed the outing and made fast friends with the Gebharts. On the other hand, I was needlessly antsy and didn't enjoy the event nearly as much as I should have. For one thing, the String Quartet just wasn't my cup of tea. I would rather have seen skinny, little Frank Sinatra.

All of this time, Mr. Gebhart, as I called him, was becoming more and more friendly with me. He was curious about my boyfriends (at school, and the kind of movies I saw. Also, at this time, I began ushering at the movie theatre occasionally when a friend, who was one of the regulars, wanted a night off. It seemed so glamorous, plus I could see a movie for free.

In addition, I had developed quite a crush on the theatre manager, Glen Dover, unbeknownst to him. But rumors were circulating that he was having an affair with the ticket box sales girl, an attractive Miss Lou Jane Smith. Glen's older, less-attractive wife, unfortunately, knew about this dalliance and became even less attractive in her bitterness.

All of us at the theatre knew what was going on between Glen and his salesgirl, and I was quite taken in by this drama. In a perverse way, I thought it made Glen even more appealing. I would hardly think that now but at the time his caddishness escaped me.

Glen and his young lady-love finally ran off together, but the marriage didn't work out. I don't know what happened to Glen's unhappy wife, but I don't think she fared well.

What might be of importance in relating this is that my emotions at that time were greatly out of control and I chose to revel in the wrong instead of the right.

CHAPTER 33

RICHARD HAD FLIRTED outrageously over the past few winter months, so it was no surprise to me when pretty Judy, who came to work as a proofreader at the newspaper, attracted Richard's roving eye also. And Richard, being the immature scoundrel that he was, relished in the on-going mutual admiration.

One Sunday the Gebharts invited Judy, whose husband was in the Army and serving overseas, to come to their house for Sunday dinner. They also asked me not as a babysitter but as a guest. I was delighted so wore my Sunday best. But it was obvious Richard would rather bestow his attentions on Judy that day, even to the point of ignoring Barbara.

I was a very young 17, and I didn't really know how to handle this development since I was accustomed to being the Gebharts' darling. This new animal on my turf completely destroyed my equilibrium.

I was peeved as dinner progressed and said very little. I knew the rejection showed on my face. So as soon as dinner was over, I busied myself with cleaning up the kitchen, though Barbara said I was a guest and didn't have to do it. I did it anyway because I felt more comfortable in the kitchen than in the living room.

All of this wasn't lost on Judy, by the way; she glowed in the attention.

When the miserable afternoon was finally over, Richard took me home. As expected, he delighted in needling me, asking, "What's wrong with you? Aren't you feeling well?"

That bastard! He was gloating and to a mere 17-year-old about his masculine prowess. Too bad I wasn't wiser; I could have saved myself a great deal of anguish and avoided this man who would so overwhelmingly go on to affect my life.

Forewarned is forearmed, they say. All the armor I had were the stern beliefs in virginity and the evils of sex. Flirtations, unfortunately, weren't included in this category of sinning. I truly thought what I was fast heading into was just a flirtation.

The day it all came to a boiling point, though, didn't come as much of a surprise. It was V-E Day—May 1945, the date the Germans surrendered, the day I surrendered my virtue, though not my virginity, not by a long shot.

I could tell that Richard was going to become more than just flirtatiously friendly. I knew he liked me; I also knew his attentions were mostly just gratifications of his emotions.

The day the Germans gave up the ghost, I was babysitting again. Classes had been dismissed for the day due to the end of the European conflict. Barbara was at a luncheon, and both the children were taking their nap when Richard came home from the office. He disappeared into the master bedroom and came out into the living room wearing his pajamas and robe.

When he said, "Jackie, come over here," I went willingly. Thus, followed my first kiss with him and, I must admit, it was even better than J.R. Clinton's that day in the laundry.

The sensation went all the way to my toes, and I could easily have collapsed. Instead, we went over to the couch which made my collapsing easier. The kiss was all that I had hoped for and all I wanted.

Getting seduced for the first time was a scary thing, in addition to being most pleasurable. I didn't consider the encounter with J.R. a seduction; it was just a kiss. However, I was unprepared for intimacy, including the discovery of massive hair I found in his pubic area when we sat down. I didn't know men could be so hairy!

There was a lot of kissing and feeling—feeling on his body, not mine—and I found it to be wonderful.

This is difficult to relate because I erased the sexual content from my mind after our first brief interlude. All I wanted to think about was the kissing, not the other part. Sex was sinful, but as long as I didn't partake of it myself, I felt I was exonerated from this tryst with a married man.

The fact that Richard was married troubled me, but not much—I was enjoying it too much. I didn't consider matrimony as an end result because I knew he would never leave Barbara for me, and I would have considered it a terrible sin if I had even slightly wished her to be out of the way. I liked her but didn't think of it as being too awful that I was romancing her husband.

Rather than labor over the entire tawdry affair, I will just say that our lovers' rendezvous, for the most part, took place in the car or at the Gebhart home when Barbara was out. Richard would find some excuse to return home before she did. I don't think she knew; at least she didn't catch us red-handed.

To someone like me, who was unpopular at school and whom the boys seemed to consider poison, I was flattered that this intelligent, handsome man was interested in me. I knew that sex was part of it, but I chose only to think of the parts I liked best—just the caressing and kissing.

Richard was 35, and I was 17, and I really don't know why he was so interested in me. He knew he was going to have an awfully difficult time getting me in bed, if, indeed, he ever did.

One night, about a month after the affair began, I went downtown to the corner on one of my rare nights off, to hang-out with the high school and junior college kids. No one ever paid much attention to me there; I just wanted the Cherry Special, so I was greatly surprised when Richard came in and sat in the booth with Billie, Mary Lou and me. He explained, as an excuse, "I've been working in the office and decided to drop by."

I don't think too many people there that night realized that he had no business being there and was risking both our reputations. Many probably never considered that the dashing Richard Gebhart would be interested in a mouse like me.

Perhaps it was a mid-life crisis he was going through, wanting to hang out with the young crowd that night. But he wasn't even middle-aged; he was still young! So, maybe he WAS attracted to me, but I tend to think his attraction was 80 percent scoundrel and 20 percent fascination.

In any case, the relationship was not a good idea and could have been very dangerous. That I wouldn't allow intercourse made it much less dangerous, but I was jail-bait for him, and he must have known it. Also, had my father known, he would have made mincemeat of Richard. No one would mess around with HIS daughters, certainly not the servicemen nor any businessmen in town.

It wasn't too difficult keeping the romance a secret, at least not for a while. Our petting sequences usually occurred on the way home in the car after babysitting, and then, when I went to work at the newspaper after the school term was over, it was much easier; especially in the editorial and advertising rooms.

The editorial room conveniently had a couch. The ad room didn't have such an accommodation, so we sat on the floor quite a bit. You notice I didn't say "laid." Even as undemanding a lover as I was, I expected to be treated with some respect and that was to recline in comfort.

This is all I can tell you about this situation in one sitting—it's too discomfiting with its indignities. I'll have to move on.

CHAPTER 34

My employment at the newspaper began on May 15, about a week after my first romantic encounter with Richard. Even though I considered myself the boss's favorite, I was still scared. I began as a proofreader; however, within a few days, Richard wanted to give me dictation.

He loved to write letters and, even more, loved to dictate them to a "secretary." It didn't matter if it was me or not; he was in his glory when he was dictating. He even called me on the phone to dictate late at night.

Having only one year of shorthand and typing didn't handicap me a great deal as a secretary. I had learned my skills well, thanks to my old home typewriter on which I practiced regularly. Even at my young age, I was a pretty good secretary.

Unfortunately, Richard would consider me as just a secretary during most of the years that I knew him. The fact that he always considered me as being no smarter or wiser than I was at 17 was evident to me in later years when

I found that the credit I thought I deserved as a writer was not, and never would be, forthcoming.

I would always be Richard's adolescent babysitter-lover-secretary who didn't need to be treated as an adult. To me, he would always be "Mr. Gebhart," never "Richard" again, not after I began working for him at the paper. Alas, this was an ill-fated relationship, and a peculiar one, composed of love/hate elements.

Barbara may have suspected there was more than just an employer-employee arrangement between Richard and me. Several instances alluded to this fact; however, I think Barbara herself was going through a mid-life crisis. As handsome and successful as her husband was, it's not unfeasible that her attention could have easily been turned in another direction. Enter Henry, the painter-carpenter-handyman.

Henry was a decent looking guy, and also in his 30s. He did handiwork for the Gebharts, was married to a Dutch immigrant, and had a sweet way with women, complimenting them and showering his attentions upon them. He didn't particularly like me—we were of the same ilk—but he certainly liked Barbara.

Barbara was not the first woman to let her mind wander into a dalliance when the glow of a marriage wore off. She was quite taken with Henry and told me so.

Once, she confided in me, "Henry's so nice and kind to me, not like Richard at all." She didn't say so, but I could see the difference in the way Henry treated her, quite a contrast to the manner of the brash, self-centered Richard.

Barbara also admitted, "I could easily have an affair with Henry."

This pleased me; I knew she wasn't concentrating on her relationship with Richard and probably didn't know about his relationship with me. So as long as Henry occupied Barbara's attention, I was safe.

But like all of God's imperfect replicas of Himself, Barbara had a mean streak and bad days. One afternoon I was helping her string beans for dinner, and she commented that she would like Janie to go away to a private school when she reached high school age, then asked me, "What do you think about it?"

What would I know about a private, rich kid's school? I felt she was trying to patronize me. I didn't like that and knew I was being put down. My good opinion of her diminished. Of course, I was bedding her husband; nevertheless, I felt righteous about the indignation.

Alas, Barbara wasn't the type to have a covert affair, and when she realized nothing would come of her admiration for Henry (and his for her), she found fault with him.

She soon realized her idol had feet of clay and was just an ordinary man. He was also too sweet and cloying and, not too long after the affair's initial inception, Barbara confided in me, "You know, Henry almost makes me sick. He's just too sweet." Thus, ended my good excuse for my immoral actions.

CHAPTER 35

MY WORK at the newspaper went well, and I liked the job. There was a lot to do and, as a junior trainee, I was schooled not only in proofreading, but subscriptions, local delivery, the cash register, and even some bookkeeping. Whatever needed to be done, the new girl was there to do it, and I did it cheerfully.

I did think I was grossly underpaid but having worked for paltry wages as a babysitter for several years; I was not equipped with the knowledge of how to obtain more money. I did, however, think my close relationship with the boss should allow me better pay than what I got. Richard apparently thought otherwise. But, in spite of this, I was a happy worker.

Then the advertising manager found out she was allergic to printer's ink—a most inconvenient malady to befall a newspaper employee. You can't avoid the stuff.

Ruth, the manager, broke out in large areas of rash on her body, and finally told Richard, "I'll have to take some time off to see if there's a remedy for this." Like everything else, the advertising duties fell to the new girl.

But I liked the work and did well for one so young. My job was to visit the downtown businesses each morning. They were parceled out on a weekly schedule, and I either made up their ads from matrixes and art work they gave me or devised them myself from our Metro Advertising Services' monthly publication.

Being an artist wasn't a requisite of the job since you could draw up an ad using the Metro service; the art work was already there to cut out, and matrixes could be found in a large box. These were used by the printers at that time to make molds by pouring hot metal over them. They were called "cuts" because they cut into the newspaper page on which they appeared.

As most people know, this was the old method of publishing a newspaper. Today's papers are offset with the efficient use of computer-generated type and ads.

With Metro and a few ideas of my own, I managed to do the job quite adequately, which pleased Richard very much—almost as much as his dalliance with me, I guess.

The business people were pleased with my work and, after a while, developed confidence in me. Of course, my pay all this time was about 50 cents an hour, which was more than I made babysitting, but I began to think I was underpaid.

I was getting bolder with the success of my job and what I thought was Richard's undying love for me. So, one day I told him I didn't think he was paying me enough.

This didn't set well with the miser, and he scoffed at the idea, saying,

"When I first met and employed Barbara on my weekly newspaper in Illinois, I only paid her a little more than I'm paying you. And she had a college degree."

I was bright enough and brash enough, to say, "Times have changed, and salaries are surely higher now than they were during Barbara's employment."

He relented and gave me a small raise per hour. He was never known for his generosity toward his employees.

Then there was the matter of Richard's drinking. I had never really been around anyone who drank a lot and when he would pick me up for babysitting or take me home later during one of his drinking bouts I was dumbfounded as to what to think about him. I attempted to humor him, but certainly didn't welcome his drunken advances, usually putting him off until he sobered up. I thought he acted quite silly.

Richard's drinking was also well-known around town since he was not merely a social drinker but an all-day tippler. Barbara also hated his drinking.

In spite of his parsimony with his employees, we all tried to protect him from public knowledge concerning his condition. He didn't drink every day, but most days. He would either come to work drunk or get drunk while he was there.

Looking back, I don't know what his problem was—he had a lovely wife, two cute children, a new home, and a successful business, but something seemed to lack in his make-up. I don't think the fact he also had me contributed to his habit since I was no real threat to him, but maybe it was a factor.

Not too many people can live in sin without feeling a

few pangs of guilt, and this guilt often brings out the worst. When I felt guilty, I had "thought trouble." So, Richard's immorality could have contributed to his drinking.

The newspaper employees denied that he drank, especially on the premises, or that he was even in the office when he was in his worst stupors. If he had telephone calls, we would just say, "Richard's not in." We didn't think he should be talking on the phone in that condition.

Also, we usually kept him in the advertising room with the door shut so no one would see him and under no circumstances would we allow him to go downtown. Some of the older employees even went to the drug store to get his liquor. (This was at least one job I didn't have to do—I was too young to buy liquor.)

I hated our affair when he was drinking since, in that state, he was obnoxious. If he had been drinking when he took me home from babysitting, I would insist on going straight inside and not to our lovers' lair.

One day at the office, he ordered me to do something, and when I retorted that he didn't need to talk to me in that tone of voice, he quickly told me, "You can just go on home."

In other words, I was fired for speaking up. So, I went home and told my parents I wasn't needed that day. However, I suspected that if I went back the next morning, he would not have meant what he said—or even have remembered it.

Sure enough, when I returned to work the next day, and after he had sobered up, he came into the ad room and said, "Did I fire you yesterday?" I told him it sounded like it; so, he immediately said he was sorry, that it wouldn't happen again. He also said, in one of his rare grandiose moods, that I was "valuable as an employee." Then he added that he thought I'd done very well in advertising for one so young and inexperienced.

Well, that helped a little too much. My fragile ego was easily inflated, so I then thought I was God's gift to men, to advertisers, and to the whole town.

I'm glad I was limited in my meandering mind when I remember even thinking, about the printers, that if they could have their choice between their dowdy wives or me, I was certain they'd pick me. Boy, does pride goeth before a fall! I was due a BIG fall!

CHAPTER 36

THE BIG FALL didn't happen right away. The summer continued its hot path in our lives, and I continued doing what I had been doing—writing and selling ads during the day, babysitting two or three evenings a week, and serving as Richard's toy. But if someone had warned me of what was to come, I would have paid no heed. I was having too much fun.

Perhaps all of this sounds as though I held Richard in disdain. That certainly was not the case; I thought I was very much in love with him.

I don't know what Richard thought and never did know. He wasn't much on sweet words; at least he didn't pander me with false hopes. In the years following, sometimes he liked me and sometimes he didn't. Richard blew hot and cold about most people, and it didn't take too big a transgression for him to feel real hatred toward the person in question.

After all these years, I think Richard was a real scoundrel for enticing a 17-year-old; he was also an asshole for all the meanness he displayed in the ensuing years. I, of course, was no lily white but, given my proclivity never to know when to say "no," I went along with the relationship and only balked when it came to down-right intercourse.

Maybe it isn't too surprising that what happened on V-J Day, August 15, 1945, did come about. Many of us remember that joyous day when World War II officially came to an end. Businesses closed, parades were held, and everyone went downtown to wave banners and yell.

The Japanese had surrendered the day before, on August 14, so August 15 was proclaimed a holiday. The newspaper wasn't published that day, and everyone was having a ball. Billie and Mary Lou wanted to take the bus to Springfield for the annual State Fair and, for once, I would have rather gone with them than to be with Richard. But Barbara had a bridge game planned that she just couldn't get out of, so Richard said he would stay with the children part of the time, relieving me so I could go to the fair.

Apparently, this was a day of celebration for Richard also, because, when he came home from the office to relieve me from babysitting, he'd had several drinks. Only the baby was at home napping; Dickie was spending the afternoon with a friend.

Richard beckoned for me to come into the master bedroom and before I knew it, he had taken part of my clothing off, and we were lying on the bed. This was an attempted rape; in no way would I consent to sex, not even then, so this was definitely forced upon me. I remember lying there, looking outdoors at the flowers in the grass, wondering how I had gotten into this mess.

Apparently, I was strong enough, and also angry enough to fight him off, and he stopped. I was indignant and insisted that he take me home right then. Although he had been drinking quite heavily, he knew he had gone too far, so he said, "I'm sorry," then proceeded to dress to take me home. Janie had not awakened during the struggle, but I told him we should get her up from her nap and take her with us.

As scheduled, I went to Springfield with Billie and Mary Lou, and we had a great time. I was quite shaken after my experience, but I was so skillful at hiding my feelings and suppressing my emotions, that I actually had a good time. I didn't feel sorry or remorseful about the predicament, but I did feel a lot of fury toward Richard. Like most attempted-rape victims, I just put the whole ordeal in the back of my mind.

I continued working in the advertising department although we knew a new director was coming in when school began in September. Then I would no longer be able to do the job, but I would, however, work half-time as an assistant.

Richard kept his distance, and I think he was more scared than sorry, afraid I might tell someone. Of course, I didn't. I didn't feel it was my fault and I seldom told anyone about my troubles, anyway. Soon we were back to our "playtime" activities.

CHAPTER 37

WHEN SCHOOL OPENED in September, it was the first year I had experienced that I didn't dread or have symptoms of another "crisis." I was actually looking forward to it, so I could brag that I had gotten a job at the newspaper that summer and would continue working part-time. I was especially anxious to tell my commercial teacher, Mrs. Gooding, that I was even taking dictation and typing Richard's letters.

That was great she said, and asked if I'd like to give a brief talk about the newspaper business and bring in samples that reflected my work. She was curious about cuts and how they were made and used, so I told her I'd bring some in.

When I told Richard, I needed some representative cuts, he said he'd find some for me. When I took them to school the next day, the girls in the class giggled when they read the ones about "piles" and other disorders of the rectum. I was quite embarrassed since I hadn't noticed the content before. When I told Richard, he laughed and said he knew the other girls would get a kick out of them.

I was hurt by the fact that he knowingly caused me embarrassment and thought *true love sure doesn't run smoothly.* Being so sensitive anyway, I wore that incident out by worrying at length about it, over and over. It should have been quite clear to me that I wasn't mature enough to handle a situation such as this, that Richard was what I already knew and repressed—an unprincipled scoundrel.

That was my senior year in high school and, as usual, I wasn't very popular. However, I assuaged my realization of this by the fact that at least I had a "lover." Hah! Some lover! Still, the thought pleased me and gave me more of a feeling of being attractive and desirable. I would have been happier if some of the boys in my class, or any in school for that matter, had desired me. But they didn't. I was just a little bit too humorless for them, with an unpleasant demeanor and a temper to match.

With the opening of school, I couldn't spend much time in the advertising department, which required a full-time employee. The new lady was very sophisticated but nice, a product of Mooresville who had spent many years in Los Angeles, only returning home to be with her ailing, aged father. Her name was Adele, and I noticed right away that, although she was older than Richard, there was a mutual attraction between the two of them. Naturally, I was jealous, but there was nothing I could do about it. Anyway, Richard's allure was losing some of its brilliance.

My new assignments at the newspaper were to help Adele with minor tasks in the advertising department, such as taking care of a few of the contract advertisers which meant that I only wrote new copy for their standard ad each week. It was also my duty to file, which naturally I hated. In addition, I eventually was assigned some duties in the editorial department.

My bad streak surfaced with the addition of Adele. None of us liked to file mats, and I'm a little astounded at my audacity when, one day, I sorted the mats I had used in my ads apart from those Adele had used. I put them in two stacks and told Adele, "Those are yours," indicating she was to file them.

Adele complained to Richard, and he admonished me, and not in a very nice way. He did let me know I could easily be replaced, that "Adele is worth 10 of you." I guess that put me in my place. I realized that illicit love-making doesn't count for much when it comes to loyalty, although expecting Richard to be loyal to me in that instance WAS unreasonable. Not long after that, I was placed in the news department.

This change boded well for me as writing news was more down my alley. I had always done well in English subjects and compositions. My first assignment was coverage of the elementary schools. I didn't have a car, but Barbara, and Richard had taught me at least the basic rudiments of driving.

I used the company car—an old Pontiac with doors that swung from the front of the car rather than the back—in driving to the schools. It was unhandy, and the car had a stick shift. Somehow, I mastered the monster. Driving it was a little like driving Mary's laundry truck.

The schools were scattered, and it would have taken up most of my four-hour work day just to get to them if I'd have walked. I soon became a familiar figure at the schools, and I thoroughly enjoyed my job. However, as I said before, the little kids emitted a universal odor. All the classrooms smelled alike. I think some ambitious entrepreneur could make a mint if he or she could concoct a good perfume for kids. Like dogs and cats, they have a definite smell.

Right away, I knew that writing, and not advertising, was my forte. I liked the contact with the public and doing little tasks such as putting names in the paper. Someone told me years later that as a news writer, I was a frustrated social worker: I liked to help others, but I always shied away from the down and dirty stuff.

A desk and typewriter were set up for me in the newsroom which housed the news editor and society editor, two women. As a mere reporter, I learned to write about obituaries, the weather, some sports scores, and even social events.

In a small town like Mooresville, social events were of the utmost importance in the newspaper, and the women who submitted accounts of the club meetings expected their work to go into the paper verbatim. One particular society doyenne, Mrs. Hoover, whom we all feared, was a tyrant and society lady from hell. If a comma were misplaced, she would call us on the phone and ream us out.

Of course, there were the uneducated and untalented writers who told us to do their write-ups in the correct manner, depending upon us to decipher their poor spelling and grammar. There were humorous contributions, also. One came from a church group at which "gum and candy were passed around for refreshments."

Ted, Barbara's younger brother, came to town in the fall. He had just been mustered out of the army and arrived for a visit before re-entering college. Ted was quite a rake, good-looking, too. Right away we summed each other up for what we really were: I knew he was a philanderer who had just left an ailing wife, and he knew I was a little tart. The first night he took me home from babysitting, he even told me, "I know what you're doing with Richard." I was surprised that it was so obvious.

Since Ted and Richard didn't like each other, they used me as the bait in their cat-and-mouse game. It goes without saying a lot of tension in the air existed between the two, and I thoroughly reveled in the attentions of both of them.

Ted definitely appealed to my emotions and, fickle to the core, I was quite enamored of him. I rationalized that at least he was accessible while Richard was an old married man. The fact that Ted was a cad didn't bother me a bit.

He was only around for a month, but he gave up on me—the eternal virgin—after a couple of weeks. When he found out I wasn't going to go to bed with him, he played his trump card: He wanted me to perform fellatio.

I was shocked and horrified. I had never heard of such a thing. Sure, I had enough aplomb not to let my fright show, but in no way would I have considered doing it. Ted realized that I was a hick who couldn't be much fun for him, so he gave up after that. I thought he was a pervert. I'm sure he recognized that I could easily become jail-bait for him, and he'd better steer clear. He didn't take me home from babysitting after that; soon he was dispatched back to his hometown in Georgia.

CHAPTER 38

THE REMAINDER of the winter and school year went by with no significant changes. Richard and I continued our playtime, and I grew further and further away from my schoolmates. I had only one friend at that time, Roxanne, and she wasn't very exciting. I didn't even hint to her about Richard. She had led such a sheltered life; she wouldn't have understood. I didn't understand the enormity of the damage I was doing to myself then, either.

I had received permission to leave school at 2:00 pm each day to go to the newspaper to continue my job there, which still encompassed news writing with emphasis on the schools. None of the boys at school asked me for a date. Since I felt I had Richard, I didn't really care.

When it came time for the annual junior-senior prom, I didn't have a date and didn't want to attend. But my parents thought I should, and Mother said she would make me a new gown. Roxanne, of course, wasn't going—it would have resulted in too much clamminess under the arms. However, some of the less-popular girls who didn't have dates either said I could go with them, and we'd stick together as one huge wallflower.

But then I encountered a problem. Stan Jones, not too popular himself, asked me to go to the prom with him. He had pimples and spaces between his teeth which completely turned me off. I didn't want to go with him at all, so I stuttered around and said I'd let him know later.

I quite preferred the company of the other unpopular girls, but I didn't know what to tell Stan to get out of going with him. Finally, I told him I wasn't going, and that I didn't like dances, all the while planning to go with the wallflowers.

When Stan encountered me at the dance with his date, he was taken aback. I told him that at the last minute that we had all gone out to dinner together, and it was just a hen party. He didn't buy that and has hardly spoken to me since, even though I've seen him at every class reunion we've had in the past 60 years.

Stan became a respected university professor with a doctorate, his complexion cleared up, but he still has spaces between his teeth. I don't know why he hasn't had them fixed; he could certainly afford to have it done. Nonetheless, he cadged onto a pretty wife and has two successful children.

Uppermost in my mind that spring, though, were plans to go to Estes Park, Colorado, with Richard and Barbara—not as Richard's paramour but as the babysitter. The occasion was a national convention of small daily newspapers with Richard slated to speak.

Going to Colorado was something I looked forward to for several months, not because of Richard but because I just wanted to go. But at the last minute, disaster struck: Dickie came down with an infected ear, so he couldn't tolerate the high atmosphere. Barbara and Richard thought they would leave the children with Richard's mother in Kansas City. I was extremely disappointed and showed it. Then they changed their plans, deciding to take little Janie and me along.

Our visit in St. Louis with Richard's mother and sister was short; we also stopped in Boulder, Colorado, to visit long-time friends of Barbara's. Then on to Estes Park, we went where the convention was held in a large resort called The Chalet.

By this time, I was not as enamored of Richard as I had once been, nor he of me. I guess true love dies when it isn't consummated, and playing little games gets wearisome after a while. He continued to kiss me and hold my hand, but I almost had the idea he was doing it because he thought I wanted him to. I would just as soon have gone without his show of affection but didn't know how to tell him

While I enjoyed the trip and only sat with Janie at night, for the most part, it was painfully obvious to me that I wasn't cut out for resorts. I didn't know how to play tennis; I wasn't athletic in any way, and I didn't make friends easily. I was shy and don't remember getting acquainted with anyone on the trip. The Gebharts, however, tried to help me have fun and, when all else failed, they suggested a horse ride up the mountain. THAT was a big mistake

I was scared of the big animal, and when the other trailwinders hastened their horses to a trot, I almost fell off mine. I managed just to hang on by pressing my upper torso against the horse's neck, holding on by the mane.

I was only comfortable when the horse slowed to a

walk, which wasn't very often. The other riders were more experienced and didn't want to wait for me. So, we jogged on with me bouncing all over the animal's back and feeling miserable. I just didn't get the hang of riding gracefully.

I was very disheveled and red-faced from the heat and strain when we returned to the stable. When Barbara asked if I had enjoyed the ride, I unconvincingly answered "yeah." But I was so tired and hot, all I wanted to do was go to bed. So much for horses.

Then Janie came down with a bronchial infection and had to be hospitalized. This occurred close to the end of our stay but delayed our departure for home. While Barbara had to stay day and night with Janie at the hospital, Richard and I were left to our own devices.

Alas, the thrill was gone. The death knell of our never-too-torrid affair in the first place began its toll. While we had most of each night available to us, naturally nothing happened between Miss Goody-Two-Shoes and her quieted lover, except to go someplace in the car and park.

It was obvious that Richard was becoming disinterested when one night at dinner he suggested I go to a movie. To make matters worse, I told him I didn't have any money. But, at least, since the hotel was within walking distance of the theatre, he was rid of me for the evening. Or to put it more concisely, I was rid of him and his pawing.

I even remember the movie—it was "Cluny Brown" with Jennifer Jones. But I don't remember if it cheered me up or not. I don't even remember if I needed cheering up. I think I was so glad to get away from Richard that I actually enjoyed myself.

That was the end of the romance. Still, since the feeling was mutual, I don't think either of us really cared, but we did manage to remain friends. And that was fortunate since I continued to work at the newspaper after we returned home.

I also managed not to get on Richard's shit-list, since those who did inevitably roused his vicious temper. He was very childish and petty enough to center all his venom on a certain employee at one time, riding that employee until he/she resigned. For all of us who worked for him, it was "beware the wrath of Richard." We knew he could destroy a person's entire persona.

I wrongly felt I came out of the debacle of our affair unscathed.

CHAPTER 39

IN 1946, we didn't call them gays and lesbians; we called them "queers." But even though I was 18, I was confused about just what a queer was. I had had conflicting information that a queer was a man who liked to do "French" kissing (putting his tongue in a woman's mouth) or have oral sex. I had also vaguely heard that he might like another man. As for women, I didn't know they could feel romantic about other women at all. Had I known, I might have been better prepared for what came next.

During my senior year in high school, a new family moved to town. I think the father was an executive in one of Mooresville's new factories. There were two daughters and one of them, Sandy, was in my class. We both had red hair and, though I later found Sandy to be much more adept socially than I, we became friends.

I soon noticed that Sandy had become friends with Marta, an attractive blond who was out of high school but had had some college. Marta was about 21 years old and worked at her father's dry cleaners. Marta and Sandy became very close, which didn't bother me since I wasn't that close to Sandy initially. The three of us sometimes went to the movies, and I thought Marta was a nice, sweet girl.

To my surprise, as soon as school was out, Sandy's parents sent her off to St. Louis for the summer. She had said little about going, and I was not expecting that development. Well, in case you didn't already suspect, Marta called and asked me to go to the movies with her, which I did. Since I had so few friends anyway, I was delighted to be asked.

She called again a few days later and not only wanted me to go to the movies with her, but I was to go as her guest, popcorn and all. That was OK, too. Marta must have been healing her bruises caused by Sandy's sudden departure since she lavished her attentions on me.

Then one night, on a walk, we had stopped for a milkshake, and she gave me a gold cross necklace. I showed my parents and they were quite alarmed; they knew what I didn't know, that Marta was not your usual, everyday 21-year-old female. It was obvious to them that she had her sights set on me, although they didn't tell me that. They just said that Marta was too old for me and that I should find other friends and leave her alone.

I was incensed. Since I didn't have a very trusting relationship with my parents, anyway, I angrily told them that every friend I'd ever had, they always found something wrong with. Vehemently, I told them I was 18 years old and had the right to pick my own friends.

They didn't issue an exact dictum but urged me to leave Marta alone. I refused but thought more seriously about it after what happened the following Sunday afternoon.

Marta had taken me for a drive in her father's car and, since she knew I didn't have an auto at the time, asked if I wanted to drive out on some country road. I thought that was a great idea and I was growing weary of that old floor stick-shift car I drove at the newspaper, so off we went. I assumed the driver's seat, and she directed me where to turn.

Marta asked me to stop, and said, "Would you mind if I kissed you?" I answered, "What?" Realizing she could blow her big chance to get intimate, she said, "Just on the cheek." That was OK, but I was having my doubts about Marta's type of affection for me. I then told her I thought we should go home, and Marta, who was smart enough not to overplay her hand, agreed. Naïve as I was, I knew something was wrong.

Fortunately, I didn't have to make a choice on my own. I didn't tell my parents about the kiss, but they adamantly didn't want things to go any further, nor did they want their daughter's reputation sullied. So, they set their foot down and said under no circumstances was I to see Marta again. I thought they were interfering too much. But I was still living under their roof, so I had to obey.

I actually liked Marta—she was kind and flattering toward me. Who could ask for more in a friend? No one else had ever paid me that much attention, so I was easily won over. I didn't want to break off the relationship in an abrupt manner. I didn't want to hurt her feelings, and I didn't want to stop seeing her.

I hedged but had to tell her my parents thought she was too old for me, that I should find friends my own age. She acted as though she was really hurt and angry, too. They were dealing with her matters of the heart. And she had her heart set on me.

Her first reaction was to woo me into a deeper relationship by buying me a pretty rose-gold flower pin and matching earrings. I said I couldn't accept the gift, that my parents wouldn't like it. She urged me to keep it hidden, that it was "just between you and me."

She also suggested we could go on seeing each other without my parents' knowledge. Well, having already learned to be a sneak with Richard, I could see the feasibility of that. But the amount of conscience I had left reared itself on little legs and told me that wasn't right. If my parents found out about any illicit meetings, I knew they would reproach me severely.

Marta and I went for walks, maybe two times after that. We unwisely stopped at the corner drug store for cokes and, since grown-ups visited the drug store on occasion, one of Daddy's cronies saw us and reported on us immediately.

After that, Mother and Daddy tried a new tactic: fear. They said they had heard Marta could be dangerous, that she might physically harm me, and under no circumstances should I see her. I think I know what they thought she would have done to me; I'm not sure what I thought, though. Sex didn't enter into the picture.

At least it didn't on my part. But Marta's hormones felt differently. To Marta's disadvantage, once rejected, her ardor for me became more profound. It was like I was the one who got away.

The next night after their warning, they went out for the evening, leaving me at home alone. They warned me not to take any calls from her or to have any contact with her should she come by.

Sure enough, here she came as soon as they left. It was an early summer evening, so I had no trouble identifying her in her dad's car. She drove by several times, slowing down in front of the house but not stopping.

I was scared, not necessarily that she would harm me physically, but, I thought, *this girl must be crazy*! So, I locked the doors and turned off the lights until she stopped driving by. Or at least I thought she had stopped; it was too dark for me to see.

I was disappointed in the outcome of the friendship, but still didn't connect sexuality, or queerness, with the way Marta might have felt for me. I avoided her after that, although the next day I encountered her in the alley between the newspaper and the cleaners, and she wanted to know if this was really the end. I said, "I have to do what my parents say. I still live there, you know."

But that wasn't the end of it–Marta joined the WAVEs. She called me at the newspaper and said the reason she'd joined was to get away from me, that I had broken her heart. Also, she said, the townspeople had been very unkind to her.

That was true. They would have been unkind to me had my parents not put a stop to our relationship. There were a lot of pseudo-Sherlock Holmes in that small town. Everyone knew what everyone else was doing. Somehow my dad was the worst of them. I don't know how I pulled it off that he didn't know about Richard. He didn't see me as a femme fatale, but as his little girl, I guess.

Anyway, Marta went to boot camp and wrote me that

she had made me the beneficiary of her will, that should something happen to her, I would receive her $10,000 in insurance. I was embarrassed and told her I didn't want the money. But, as affairs of the heart go, she fell out of love with me, and I'm sure at some point I was taken out of her will.

For reasons which may be explained later, I suffered an extreme siege of guilt about my relationship with one who was far more advanced in years than I. That was a phase of my life for which I was fully unprepared and blameless. I didn't know that, though, until much later. I wish my parents had taken me aside and explained exactly what was going on; it would have saved me a lot of grief.

But there are always "what if's." I could have been born to my Uncle Manfred and had a much different life; I could have been born to other parents not half as good as mine. My parents were who they were, and I was lucky to have them, in spite of their mistakes.

CHAPTER 40

THE SUMMER WENT BY unremarkably. Richard and I distanced ourselves from each other more and more. I was growing up; he was growing tired (of me). Since my friendship with Marta didn't reach the depths of erotica, I soon felt little loss when I realized I had to leave her alone.

I continued working at the newspaper, writing news in the mornings and taking Richard's correspondence and other business affairs in the afternoon. I also had an arrangement with him that when the local junior college opened in the fall, I could continue working half-time.

As we were getting into post-war, the veterans returned to civilian life, many of them quite young who had gone into service fresh out of high school or who had interrupted their college careers. With the new GI Bill of Rights, many of them wanted to take advantage of the free education offered rather than going back to a menial job or drifting from one thing to the next.

One of the returning GI's from nearby Piersall took my

eye: Don Ward, worked part-time at one of the local grocery stores. He was three or four years older than me, but, alas, my admiration for him was not reciprocated. He had his sights set on a little girl from Piersall, so my flirtations went for nothing.

However, as a favor for a friend, he came along on a double date one night with another couple and me. I found myself in the uncomfortable position of being the unwanted fourth party.

The other couple consisted of Morris Collins and Polly St. Andrews, the daughter of our new church minister. Morris arranged the date, but from the start, it was obvious that Don couldn't have cared less about going out with me. He would much rather have been with the object of his affections from Piersall. But since I was staying overnight with Polly while her parents were out of town for a few days, he agreed to come.

He certainly did me no favor. In fact, he was quite rude to me and being the shy violet that I was, I suffered through the insult when a more confident girl would have asked why he had come along in the first place.

Polly, who was madly in love with Morris—and married him a few months later—was so lovesick that when we went to bed, she hugged me all night and cooed and crooned about the wonderful Morris. I didn't appreciate being a surrogate for him and wished I had never agreed to the minor debacle.

Also, Polly proved to be a very insensitive girl when it came to my feelings. She blithely said, "Well, I guess you and Don didn't hit it off. But maybe next time you'll be as lucky as I am." I decided right then and there that I didn't want any more arranged dates. Even Richard, who no longer loved me (if he ever did), was more considerate of my feelings than Don had been.

CHAPTER 41

SO MUCH for summer romance. When classes opened at the junior college in September, Don was there, but we ignored each other. However, when classes began in September at the college, there was one returning serviceman who thought I was a pretty cool cookie. His name was Harry Bowen, and I remembered him from when he was a senior, and I was a freshman in high school. Harry had a couple of classes with me, and he was quite nice looking—dark curly hair, dark-lashed blue-gray eyes, and a pretty smile. He was small, though—about my height as long as I didn't wear heels. But I was glad to overlook that.

The first date he asked me for was to attend the local high school football game, which I didn't understand a whit. But I liked the excitement of the fall air, the cheerleaders, the marching band, even the drum corps.

Harry arrived in a used auto he had purchased since returning that past summer and, while it wasn't new, it was nice enough. The first thing I noticed about him, and which enticed me, was his fresh smell of soap and an after-shave with which I wasn't familiar. Since I hadn't been going out with "boys," only "men" (like Richard), I was unfamiliar with how they were supposed to smell. To me, Harry smelled quite delicious.

He was friendly and talkative and quickly pried me out of my shell. I noticed I was enjoying myself. He had been with the Army in the European Theatre, spending quite a lot of time in Italy. Naturally, he had a girlfriend over there, but I wasn't too worried about her. I was here and available, and that made me feel better.

What intrigued me most was his description of Italian food, much of which I didn't know about because Italian food hadn't been particularly popular in my growing-up years. I guess I had eaten Franco-American spaghetti from a can, but that was about the extent of it.

Harry told me about "cheese pie" which he called "piestza" and which later became "pizza" to the American public. The Italian variety that Harry had eaten had cheese and sometimes a sliced tomato on it, but all the glop that's put on it as we know it today was largely American-inspired. Perhaps the Italians added the first pepperoni, but I think the Americans can take credit for the mushrooms and anchovies.

Harry intrigued me, and I seemed to intrigue Harry. Before long we were a regular twosome, and I thought I was in love with him. He stirred me inwardly, but I did notice he tended to be quite conceited. Granted, he was good-looking, but he could have stood to be a tad taller. Also, as I soon learned, he was the only boy in a family of four and had been greatly spoiled, especially by his mother.

I also soon realized that Harry's oldest sister, Helen,

had been my sixth-grade teacher, the one who caught me cribbing that unfortunate day when I blatantly looked up all the test questions in the text book. If she remembered the incident or said anything to Harry about it, I didn't know. It was tactfully never mentioned.

Harry's other sisters were Ruth, an always-fat girl who never married and who sublimated whatever sexual drives she might have had by finishing her doctorate and becoming a college professor. Then there was young Joyce, not a pretty girl but decidedly sexy as she grew older. Joyce had no trouble getting boyfriends, or husbands either. I think she had two or three.

CHAPTER 42

HARRY'S MOTHER doted on her only son, and the subsequent spoiling showed up at times. It was not serious, but enough to cause me considerable grief. I worried a lot about our relationship, asking myself "Does he really love me or is he just a charmer?" Or, "Does he have other girlfriends on the nights I don't see him?" Being insecure made it difficult for me to trust him, and my poor self-image made me wonder at times what he really saw in me.

As usually happens with red-blooded young Americans, especially those young men who had been in the service and had had a taste of camaraderie, the two of us drifted into a foursome.

I told Harry, "My friend, Sandy, who went to St. Louis for the summer, has come back and is enrolled in the college. Would you like to have her, and her boyfriend go out with us sometime?"

"Yes," Harry answered. "That would be nice."

Sandy was in a romance with another returning veteran, Howie Waters. In my opinion, he was a bit of a wimp and a little on the stupid side. I told Harry, "I don't know what Sandy sees in him," but Harry retorted, "He's OK and easy to get along with." So, we became a foursome.

Having been scathed by Sandy's disregard for me when she left me in Marta's care, I should have been forewarned that she could be bad news. But in the meantime, she wasn't and seemed completely wrapped up in Howie.

My relationship with Harry became very close, and I liked him a lot. I didn't go out with any of the other guys, but I was friendly with a number of them. I seemed to have more in common with the older ones than the boys my own age. Of course, I was a very serious-minded young lady and had always been a little too severe for boys in my class. I just wasn't any fun for them.

Then I began to see little mean traces in Harry. As a high school graduation gift, I had received a phonograph, semi-automatic, or as automatic as they knew how to make them in 1946. My favorite record was "I Cover the Waterfront." I almost wore it out by playing it over and over again. Then one unfortunate night when I was playing records for our little foursome, someone stepped on "Waterfront" and broke it.

I was heartbroken. Harry, however, wasn't particularly concerned; in fact, he laughed and proceeded to tease me about it. Right then I decided he was a cold turd.

I should have been smart enough then to branch out to some of the other young men, especially some of those who were so friendly with me in study hall and the coffee room. But I didn't. I thought Harry was the only one for me, in spite of his sometimes, arrogant disregard for my feelings. I wasn't even aware that some of the other guys wanted to take me out, but later learned they did. As we definitely know by now, my confidence in my charms was still in the negative. However, I did see a few sparks of interest but thought they only wanted to be friends.

CHAPTER 43

EVIL COMES OUT during the usual doldrums of a dreary January. It came out in Harry that January.

One night, upon returning home from the movies, Harry didn't make another date with me but just said, "I'll see you later." At the college when I met him in the hallways, he was distant, and it was obvious I was getting the old heave-ho. I was stunned.

Actually, Harry was prudent in what he was doing: monogamy only belongs in marriage or to the engaged. We hadn't entered that realm and, having just given three years of his life to the military; I suppose Harry was beginning to think it was a little too soon to tie himself to an immature, small-town girl. No doubt, there were other blossoms to pluck.

I, too, should have realized this was my first "true love," that there were other fish in the sea. But such is the matter of the insecure heart: I was bereft.

Then the final blow: He asked Sandy to go out with

him. Poor wimpy Howie and I were left empty-handed and, since neither of us thought the other was attractive, we didn't find much consolation in each other. We did talk at length about how badly we had been burned, and about how we could get even. But the truth was, we didn't know how to get even, nor did we really want to.

This rejection doused my already fragile ego, and I saw it as a big defeat. I was sure my life was ruined. I went to classes and half-heartedly worked at the newspaper. Then I would go home and go to bed. I didn't eat.

My parents knew what ailed me; it was obvious to them that Harry wasn't coming around anymore. I also reluctantly told them he was dating Sandy. They were very sympathetic about all this, trying to pep me up with advice such as "He isn't worth all this grief. Let him have Sandy, who isn't as pretty as you are in the first place."

My mother sagely advised me, "Two can play the same game. There are other young men out there, and you certainly don't owe Harry anything."

All this landed on deaf ears, and I continued to mope about the house. If my classmates knew what was going on with me, they didn't let it be known. And none of the other guys were exactly pounding at my door to get in. Likely, though, Miss Mopey didn't exude much charm at the time.

Just as I was beginning to come out of my stupor, though, Harry did me the questionable favor of realizing he liked me better than he did Sandy. There was to be a Valentine's Day dance, so one day in the hallway, Harry actually stopped me to talk. He said, "About the Valentine's Day dance, would you like to go with me?"

I should have said "No" or hedged at least a little, but did I? Of course not. I was delighted and said, "Yes, I would."

My parents didn't like this change of events and told me, "Beware of Harry."

I had to admit they were right. While all seemed well on the surface, I didn't immediately forget what Harry had put me through. In the back of my mind was forming a little oyster pearl of distrust and resentment. While I may not even have admitted it to myself, I knew I'd get even.

CHAPTER 44

NOT QUITE so trusting after the Sandy episode, I began to notice that Harry was a little flakey. He had often complained that his father had always been a dreamer, never settling down to one thing for long. He did have a good position with an oil company and lived at what we called the "Gulf" in one of the nice company-owned houses southeast of town.

One day Harry told me, "Dad has often come up with some hare-brained idea on how to get rich quick, but I notice he's always careful to keep his secure position with the oil company."

One such get-rich-quick scheme presented itself at about the close of the college year in May. Mr. Adams decided that he and Harry would go into the processed chicken business as soon as Harry was free of classes. I don't know how much input Harry had in this matter, but at the end of the college year they set up their business in an old downtown building with some used equipment.

Their chicken operation included killing the chickens,

gutting them, taking off the feathers, and either cutting them up or packing them whole for roasting. All of this was to be done in a hot, smelly, uncomfortable, and, what smacked of unsafe and unsanitary conditions, during the steamy months of the summer. They did, of course, have refrigeration and, as far as I know, didn't sell or deliver any spoiled or otherwise defective chickens.

It didn't seem like a very smart method to get-rich-quick. But if diligence insures success, at least the first two months of the summer, father and son should have been quite happy with their efforts. That is if they had had time to pursue any of the pleasures of life on which to spend their hard-earned money. They worked night and day and, when I did see Harry, he was usually too tired to be any fun.

The new schedule seemed to be right up Harry's alley—it gave him the opportunity to aggravate me more by never knowing when, or if, at the last minute he could keep a date, or we could do something. I was beginning to feel if he preferred the smell of chickens to my dainty Faberge Woodhue, let him have at it. I didn't cry anymore or take to my bed over his macho antics.

For one thing, I had girlfriends! That was something new for me. But I found comfort with the girls who were often having similar male-related problems, especially from the war veterans who were either neurotic from shellshock or greatly impressed with themselves for having saved the world. So, we took comfort in each other's big problems of the moment—namely men and clothes.

We were the girls who spent our first year of college at the local junior college, most of us for financial reasons. I didn't mind this at all because I wasn't ready to leave home; also, I had my job at the newspaper which I liked very much, and wanderlust hadn't gotten hold of me at that time.

In addition to boys and clothing, our other thread of friendship was sewing. All of us who were left behind had this in common: We were old-fashioned enough to be working on our "hope chests."

We met at each other's homes about once a week and took our embroidery or whatever our project was at the time. I made a very pretty light blue luncheon set with white cross-stitch, and I was so obsessive about it, I made sure all the cross-stitches were stitched in the same direction. I didn't miss many, and, if I did, I went back and corrected them. My habit was in full-force, but I was also so accustomed to trying to be perfect.

My morals were in full-force, too. I was Miss Goody-Two-Shoes in those days and never took a drink and wouldn't have dared smoke a cigarette. I was just too pious for any of those nasty habits. I had grown out of my flirting-with-older-men stage, also, and contented myself at that time with Harry.

I was also the perennial virgin. I could have even beaten good old Doris Day at her game. The fact that I still held Richard's hand once in a while and gave him an occasional kiss didn't seem to count.

But the other girls in the group didn't know this side of me. If they had, I'm sure they would have been intrigued. However, I kept my sins well hidden. I was a good church-goer, but don't ask me what I thought religion was all about, except to be good. I never did learn the names of the books of the Bible like most of the other Sunday

School attendees did. I thought that was nonsense; what possible good could that do me?

The other girls included Ruth Ann, whose rich Swedish-American farmer parents sent her to Mooresville High School rather than their little school in the nearby burg of Avondale, so she could get a better education. Rich as they were, though, they didn't want Ruth Ann to go away to college because she was their baby (after four sons), and they wanted to keep her at home.

There was also Roxanne, the over-protected daughter of neurotic parents who didn't want her to attend public school for fear she'd pick up germs.

Dorothy, one of my life-long friends from kindergarten, also stayed back as did Phyllis, another offspring of wealthy parents who simply wasn't mature enough to leave home. (Many years later I saw her quite often in our mutual psychiatrist's office. I don't know what her problems were.)

And there was Beatrice, a large girl who was quite pretty but hadn't the least bit of confidence or poise that would have been expected of an 18-year-old.

We, young seamstresses, had fun, and I loosened up. Since my earlier experience with the vicious Sylvia and Jeanie, I hadn't really been involved with more than one girlfriend at a time, so I enjoyed this new fertile field of companionship. They also helped me cope with Harry; I discovered that he wasn't the omnipresent factor in my life and that there were other fish in the sea. I soon found them.

CHAPTER 45

DURING ALL THIS "growing-up" time with Harry, the habit was still present but not as profound. I had many doubts about myself—and certainly a lot about Harry— but I was actually having fun and felt a little more independent, not as child-like under the strict thumb of my parents.

Mother and Daddy seemed to accept the fact that I was dating and were relatively sure that I wasn't going to do anything wrong (or sinful.) They believed they had raised me well with the proper moral codes as well as a big enough fear of pregnancy that I wouldn't be crawling into the back seat of a car at the first invitation.

I still believed in retaining my virginity, though I had slackened my rigidity of my puberty days a bit. Harry respected my youth and strict parents in that he never pressured me to have sex. We did, however, do some heavy petting close to the end of that first summer, but, fortunately, it went nowhere.

Harry was not particularly popular with my parents

and Billie. They thought he treated me badly, especially during his romance with Sandy. However, realizing that I liked him a lot, they remained quiet on the subject. Billie, however, was not so gracious; she was quite cool to Harry, but in his conceit and ignorance, he didn't seem to notice.

Once, while feeling his oats and bantering about his charms, he told me, "You know, I have 'maggotism.'" Of course, he meant "magnetism" but wasn't smart enough to even know how to pronounce it. Since I was beginning to see through him, I enjoyed his mistake and gleefully told Billie.

We had a good laugh out of that, and it was a standing joke between us for several years, especially when the other got a little uppity or vain. We would remind each other that "you've got a bad case of maggotism."

Poor Harry. He should never have sought to get away with anything with sisters who were as close as Billie and me. We had a lot of private laughs at others' expense.

CHAPTER 46

I REALIZED I was getting close to the end of childhood and embarking on adulthood. Harry was helping me grow up quite speedily with his quirks and mercurial personality. I was certain I wasn't going to let him hurt me again as he had with Sandy. I became closer to Billie, and our good friend, Annie, and the three of us enjoyed many mirthful moments. Harry was the subject of some of them.

As is often the case, we think as we're growing up that we have the worst lot in life of any of our classmates or friends, but when we look back on it, as the three of us often did in adulthood, it was the best time of our lives; especially growing up in a small town such as we did.

We knew many people; we were accepted; we had fun, we had sorrows, but, all in all, it was a great time. Difficult as I thought my childhood was, I wouldn't change much– except for the "crises" which I attribute to a mental illness that no one understood in those days.

One of the problems of my growing up was that it was during the era of the nouveau-movie age. I was highly impressed with what I saw on the screen. It provided a background with which to compare what I thought was my droll, tragic life. I thought of myself as an infantile Scarlet O'Hara to whom diversity was a challenge and that someday "I'd show them."

Or I saw myself as a character in a book or movie as I was growing up and was very impressed by what I saw in the films. I don't think I would have absorbed such explicit images had I relied upon books to educate me about the vagaries of life. The movies were bigger and much more dramatic.

Primitive as most of them were as entertainment, they were advantageous in that we learned about other modes of living and other parts of the world. But they also made us dreamers, dreamers of much that we could not attain. Television doesn't have that impact upon us today...we're over-exposed to it.

At any rate, I'm going to finish off Harry, and I do mean finish him off. I never forgave him for that fling with my so-called best friend. But in his own little egotistical mind, he thought I was ever-loving and, probably, stupid.

But with the end of Harry, regretfully came the end of my childhood.

Richard, Harry and what few dalliances I had had didn't rob me of my innocence, nor ruin my childhood. That little orange book did. I knew too much, too soon.

CHAPTER 47

WHEN I MET WARD, he provided sweet revenge for me against the errant Harry.

The two of them lived in the same area southeast of town, and when Ward and a friend, Gene, came on the scene, Harry introduced me to this brown-eyed wonder who looked like Perry Como. While I was not taken by him at first, his relaxed, cool manner appealed to me as did the sultry look in those chocolate eyes.

However, I was surprised a few nights later when Ward called me, asking me to go for a drive and get a coke. I had just washed my hair and, in those days when we didn't have home dryers, I couldn't possibly have gone out with wet hair.

Ward wasn't too sure I wasn't just putting him off, and said, "I guess you're going steady with Harry so maybe I shouldn't have called you."

I said, "No, I'm not Harry's girlfriend, and I would like

to go out another time. Really, my hair is very wet, so I can't go tonight."

I should have asked him to call a day ahead of time, but my self-confidence in alluring young men wasn't sufficiently developed to make such restrictions. So, when he called a week later inviting me to a movie, I accepted, even though I had little notice.

It was at this time that Harry, without a word to me or even asking me if I minded, took a job with Western Electric as an electrical wire installer and unceremoniously left for Alabama. No doubt, his venture with his dad in the chicken business hadn't made them rich, so it was easy to give up.

The point is that he announced he had taken a job, that he wasn't going back to college, and he expected me to wait for him until he got settled, and then, MAYBE, we'd get married. He hadn't proposed, and I had made no promises, but I think the two of us understood that our relationship was leading down to the altar.

He didn't ask me if I wanted to live in Alabama, if I wanted to quit my job, quit school, and leave my parents. In his egotistical mind, it wasn't necessary to ask—he told me. But I was a little miffed, so when Ward called, I was only too happy to go out with him.

I liked Ward immediately. He was easy-going, not at all excitable like my dad, and suave. I think the fact that he was seven years older attracted me also since it gave him a somewhat paternal aura which I needed. I had never had an affectionate relationship with my own father and felt I could lean on Ward. I certainly didn't feel that way about the selfish Harry.

There was another factor as well: Ward was also dating one of Ruth Ann's good friends, Andrea Gail, who lived nearby. Andrea was a pretty girl, also with brown eyes, and I thought she and Ward were quite serious.

Apparently, they weren't, although Ward continued to date her and me at the same time. I was jealous of Andrea, but it gave me a masochistic glee to imagine her romance with Ward. I wondered if she was as jealous of me as I was of her. The fact that I could take someone's boyfriend away from her gave me a decidedly wicked joy. (I'm ashamed to admit that. I always thought I had higher moralistic leanings.)

When Harry came home after a little more than a month in Alabama, on Labor Day weekend, I was quite smitten with Ward and wasn't especially happy to see Harry. In fact, he bored me a little in addition to the fact that I was piqued with him for having made his decision about Alabama without even consulting me. However, I did spend my free time during the entire holiday weekend with him, but not joyously.

Harry noticed the change in my demeanor and asked, "Is something wrong? Are you mad at me?"

I told him, "Perhaps you know I've been dating Ward since we met that day at the swimming pool, but we're just friends." Well, he didn't like that one little bit, but, since he had no real strings on me, there was nothing he could do.

CHAPTER 48

WARD DIDN'T EXACTLY RUSH me and seemed to be taking his time in deciding between the beauteous Andrea and me. He was French-Italian and, like most men of that background, had a certain Old-World aura which was appealing. He was a little bit of a tease, too, and liked to joke.

Had I been older and wiser, I might have wondered why a young man of 26 didn't work. I soon learned, too, that Ward lived on a farm with his widowed mother, and that apparently the two of them farmed their 80-acre spread. He was also attending school on the GI Bill.

Had I been smarter, I would have questioned myself, *would I genuinely like farm living, and do I want to spend the rest of my life as a farmer's wife?*

As I was quite enamored of Ward, I didn't give these notions a thought. I was a very young 19. So, I went blithely along, accepting dates of movies or going to the only area place for young people to gather—the old Westport Inn south of town.

Most of the college students, returning veterans, and girls who were old enough, went to Westport to dance to the jukebox. Apparently, we were allowed to drink beer at age 18, so I started drinking a little. Ward was not much of a drinker either, but I'm sure beer was the drink of the day.

At home, occasionally, my dad would fix me a highball after I returned from work at the newspaper, but, strangely, he didn't want me to drink coffee. I guess that would have been admitting that I had really grown up.

In the meantime, I continued to date Ward and write to old Harry, and I wasn't getting serious about anyone or anything. I had also started my second year of junior college, working part time at the newspaper as a reporter. My bad thoughts weren't plaguing me at that time, not even with the beginning of the school year when I was usually afflicted.

CHAPTER 49

AT THIS TIME ALSO, Billie was in her first year at the junior college, and she and Annie, who was two years younger, had become quite good friends. Annie's father was probably the wealthiest merchant in town, owning a fruit and vegetable produce business with a fleet of trucks in the nearby three-state area.

Annie's father and our dad were great friends, so our parents started going away together on weekends, leaving Billie and me to stay with Annie in the family's large Tudor-style house. We called it a "mansion." It had five bedrooms and was centered on a full city block. It wasn't a mansion but was one of the most impressive homes in the town.

So, my social life was blooming, and into it came another attraction—Chauncey Gates from Carterville, about 20 miles south of Mooresville. He was a friend of Mary Lou's boyfriend, Calvin, and came up to see me quite often after I met him in September. One day he drove up in a spanking-new car which his brother-in-law had just purchased. Since this was just after the war, new cars were a novelty, and I was quite impressed with that maroon number; Chauncey as well.

Chauncey's father was rich, also, and Chauncey was just a little spoiled, but he was nice. The only problem was that he was about my height and I dared not wear heels, into which I had grown since I didn't want to diminish his height any further. But I liked him, even though I began to notice he was quite a drinker—certainly more than I was accustomed to being around.

The young people hung out at a nightclub called the Parakeet, and the drinking was more than just the regulatory beer of Westport since mixed drinks were also served.

People much older than we were went there and, while my parents didn't like the idea of their daughters rubbing shoulders with such a "rough" crowd, they knew we were growing up. They were trusting us to use a little common sense. Neither of us drank much, anyway.

But there was the other side of the coin to Chauncey— he DID drink quite a bit; in fact, way too much for his small stature. One night we went with Mary Lou and Calvin in Chauncey's own car, a new Buick coupe. He proceeded to lace his beer drinks with highballs, and pretty soon he became quite drunk and then disgustingly sick.

Calvin told me, "I think you'd better take him to the car before he gets severely drunk and sick."

Unfortunately, he was already that way and as soon as we got to the car, he chucked up on his socks and was miserable. I wasn't accustomed to such uncouth behavior, so I wasn't at all sympathetic.

Poor Chauncey. He knew he had blown it with me so,

instead of going to sleep like most drunks would, he dissolved into a litany about how "no-good" he was. Guilt was also attacking him, and he continued telling me how sorry he was, at the same time regaling himself for being "an asshole, just a no-good drunk."

He went on running himself down until I began to think it was funny. Laughing at him didn't necessarily cheer him up, though. I'm sure he was quite happy when Mary Lou and Calvin came to mercifully drive us home.

This wasn't the end of our relationship, however. While I was very forgiving, I wasn't quite so enamored of him after that. I compared him to the suave Ward, who would never have acted that childishly. Unfortunately, as I was to find out, Ward was never sorry for anything he did anyway, and after the ardor wears off, a decent apology can have a big appeal in a relationship.

CHAPTER 50

BUT BACK to poor Hapless Harry. He knew I was cooling toward him, also that he was being irrevocably replaced by Ward. So, he put on the sympathy act, telling his relatives and our friends how I was letting him down and hurting him. Also, word got around that he was planning to give me an engagement ring for Christmas.

My three-pronged heart put up with Harry until Christmas and, ironically, I got all three of my current boyfriends, including Ward and Chauncey, the same gift—small gold pen knives. And they all three bought me the same thing— expansion gold watch bands for the watch my parents had given me for graduation. Of course, I had hinted ignobly that that was what I wanted, so that's what I got.

And Heartbroken Harry got something else he didn't want—his walking papers. I happily broke off our relationship and was glad to be rid of him. But he let it be known among all our mutual acquaintances that while he was off trying to aggrandize our future life together, I was in fact "laying out," as my dad always called our relationships with boys.

Harry painted me as the scarlet woman of the year. But I didn't care. I was having fun, so the hell with Harry. I also thought he got what he deserved.

CHAPTER 51

AFTER CHRISTMAS, life quieted down somewhat. Heartless Harry went back to Alabama, licking his wounds, and Chauncey resumed classes at the university. He had stayed out the first semester, for whatever reason I don't know. Probably bad behavior.

I continued seeing Ward the Wonder who had had some sort of understanding with Andrea: "This relationship isn't going anywhere," she told him, and he alluded to the fact that, "Well, I've found someone else I like better." (Ward was not known for his tactfulness.)

But then trouble began. Ward became more sexually aggressive and thought he had spent enough time with me that his male ego should have been rewarded with sex. Ward always had a number of buddies hanging around, and, in his Old-World culture, it was a star in the male's crown to have proved his sexual prowess with his woman of the moment.

I'm sure Ward and his buddies discussed their conquests with each other; and, after spending the whole of six months with a girl, felt it was time that the relationship was consummated.

When he began pushing for a sexual relationship, I adamantly refused. He didn't mention love or marriage or how he needed and wanted me. It was more or less that it was just time we did it.

In my pious little mind, I told him, "I've never done it and don't intend to until I'm married."

He scoffed at this. "Don't tell me you never did it with Harry. I know him, and the two of you certainly went together long enough."

No amount of argument on my part could convince him that I was still a virgin, so I quieted down on the matter. I was still dating a few of my college classmates from time to time, but none of the affairs were serious. I was busy with my college studies and working half-days at the newspaper, but I could recognize that trouble was seeping in where it shouldn't have.

Ward was seven years older than me, and I was a very immature 19-year-old. The fact that he didn't respect my religious and moral values should have warned me that he was the wrong guy for me. Had I been able to see beyond his good looks and charm, I would have known he was a cad.

CHAPTER 52

AT ABOUT THIS TIME, someone else came into my life, though I hardly realized it was happening and paid little attention to him. For one thing, I didn't see how this nice young man, Bill Annis, could be interested in a small-town girl like me. Maybe he wasn't sure I'd be interested in him either because he certainly held back his attentions until it was almost too late for us even to get acquainted.

Bill was in Mooresville with two associates from a fund-raising company based in Kansas City. Bill's dynamic firm was a respectable, legitimate and successful organization. They weren't fly-by-night entrepreneurs hoping to make a buck off small-town naïve citizens.

The other two young men were both married but Bill, who also turned out to be seven years older than me, was single. He was, I was to find out later, reluctantly involved with the local Chamber of Commerce secretary Gerry Barr, who either forced her attentions on Bill or he was too nice a guy to hurt her feelings by letting her know he wasn't interested. Most of us in town thought the two were involved since they did spend a lot of time with each other.

I wasn't at all aware that Bill had noticed me quite often in my comings and goings at the newspaper, which was located across the street from his office in the Chamber of Commerce area of City Hall.

However, one day in the back shop of the paper, I was busy using the stapling machine on some pamphlets which had just been printed and were scheduled to go out. While my duties at the newspaper were mainly writing, I had to do various and sundry other tasks that are usually relegated to the youngest and least important person on the staff. I didn't like it but put on a good front and took it as my due.

Bill came into the newspaper office and walked back to the shop where he saw me laboring away. He said, "What are you doing there?"

I good-naturedly answered, "This is really manual work I'm doing, but there's no one else to do it."

He thought that was funny since I was quite small to be using such a big apparatus, then said in his shy way, "I'm leaving Saturday, you know, and wondered if we could go to the movies Thursday night?"

Unfortunately, I had plans with Ward that Thursday and couldn't go, so he asked, "Well, I'd like to get to know you better. Could we write to each other?"

I was flattered and answered, "Of course," but wondered silently why he had taken so long to pay me the compliment of wanting to know me better.

So, I gave him my address and thought very little about

him. He left on Saturday and after he arrived home in Indianapolis, immediately wrote to me. He apparently lived in an affluent area with his widowed mother, but that was really all I knew.

I was to grow to know him much better, and he became a much more important factor in my life than I would have ever thought. We wrote to each other often, and I enjoyed his intelligent letters. It was obvious that he was well-educated. I even learned some new words, like "obstreperous," which he said I was. I had to look it up in the dictionary, and I suppose I was that way, but I actually thought I was just being cautious. I wasn't at all trustful of male intentions, thanks to Richard and even Ward.

Unfortunately, Bill came during the beginning of another mental crisis, though we continued our friendship through a period in which my mental condition worsened. And I regret that he didn't come along sooner than he did. Perhaps he could have saved me from the turn my life took, long before I was ready to be pummeled into the adult world I was eventually forced to face.

CHAPTER 53

WARD CONTINUED pushing me for sex. Always having taken life situations quite seriously, this matter didn't escape my worrisome mind either. I was still cheerful and believed in my state of "goodness" until one night it suddenly dawned on me that I MIGHT have had sex—with Richard.

Although I had put it completely out of my mind, that V-J Day incident came back full score to haunt me, and I wondered: *did Richard really succeed when he tried to force intercourse on me?* Also, I thought, *just how far did he go?* (Had I known the word, I would have thought "penetrate.")

Well. Here was another crisis...and a very serious one. This was no small overnight worry for me. It became an obsession and, given my confused state of mind, it was a major obsession.

All of a sudden, I changed from a cheerful, out-going, carefree young girl to a worried, guilt-ridden, concerned shadow of my former self. Nothing seemed funny anymore. Nothing was enjoyable. School was a burden and seeing Richard at the newspaper was not only agonizing but distasteful.

I've read that people with obsessive-compulsive disorder waste about one-third of their time worrying or "processing" things. I did just that. In quiet times, when I would come home from work, it looked like I was reading the paper, but actually, I was going over and over in my mind what had happened that August 15. It became a horrifying specter for me and, could I have gotten away with it, I would have screamed out in agony.

The thoughts were so vivid and horrible that I made myself ill pondering them. My dad especially noticed the change in my personality and said, "Is something bothering you? You've been awfully quiet lately." *How could I tell him? How could I possibly tell anyone?*

My thoughts ranged from the fact that maybe my hymen had been broken in that incident. (Hymens seemed to be of some importance in those days, although it was often explained that the hymen could be broken by riding a horse, playing sports, or vigorous activity.)

I could imagine all kinds of ways that it could be broken, but the most frightening thing to me, for a few days at least, was that it might have happened when Richard tried to force intercourse on me.

I was very ignorant about sex, and it seems the less I knew, the more frightening the incident. I didn't want to ask questions because I didn't want anyone to know I was so concerned about sex. Even asking would have marked me.

Then it occurred to me that Richard was a *married* man! And to have had your first sexual experience with someone married was like, well, having it with your own father, who of course, was also married! Although in no way did my father ever even hint of sexuality to me, it was still another frightening and horrible aspect to think about. That thought alone made me want to tear my hair out.

All this time, I was in school and working at the newspaper, still functioning but not well. My grades were slipping, and I wasn't as interested in going out with Ward or to the sewing parties with my girlfriends. The job was just a job. I more or less went through the motions of it like a zombie. My thoughts turned inside out.

As it seems to be God's way when no other help is available, the mind can't stand anymore, and it stops. The matter isn't resolved, but it can be pushed to the rear. But with that relief came a small sort of "walking break-down." I was a very disturbed girl.

I became almost physically ill in addition to being quite nervous. On my parents' advice, I went to our family doctor who gave me some medicine for my nerves. I calmed down enough to halfway pull myself together. I got in stride with my studies, managing to put the bad thoughts in the background, and continued my relationship with Ward.

I also began to spend more of my time with Billie and Annie, and Bill Annis wrote me from Kansas City, inviting me up for a visit with him and his mother. I went places with my girlfriends more, although I missed a couple of parties simply because I just didn't feel up to going.

My production on the job improved and, for a while, I thought I was getting over this specter about Richard. But I was sad. I no longer felt like I was a "good girl." No, I felt like a harlot. Life was empty.

I was carrying around a giant-sized guilt complex about my affair with Richard. The big question in my mind, which I had learned to keep under control, so I could go about my usual activities, was, "Did he do it or not?" It was very important to me that he DIDN'T do it!

This thought made me even more adamant about not having sex with anyone, certainly not the pressuring Ward. Fortunately, he wasn't physically aggressive, so he didn't try to force me, but he was verbally consistent.

Since we had no real understanding about our future, and never talked about it, he didn't seem to mind that I went out with other young men. He evidently knew I wasn't going to be promiscuous with any of them so, at least, his male ego wasn't challenged.

Ward was also smart enough to know he had no ties on me and that I was free to date whomever I pleased. I don't know about his other alliances at the time, but his relationship with Andrea was over. If he went out with other girls, I didn't know about it, nor did I think about it.

I liked one student at junior college, John Bennett but I only had one date with him. He had already been smitten by a high school junior and, while he was polite to me, it was obvious he wasn't overly impressed. He later married his high school junior.

I also dated a young man who came from Alabama to visit one of the War Moms he had known during wartime while he was stationed at the nearby Army camp. Mrs. Taylor, his hostess, was a friend of my mother's and told her, "I think Jackie would be just the ticket for Charles when he comes for a visit. Do you think she'd be interested?"

Mother said, "I don't see why not. She doesn't go with Ward all the time but has dates with other boys."

When we met, I was impressed with Charles' good looks, and he apparently thought I wasn't bad either. We hit it off rather well and liked each other immensely. But I was so unsure of myself, as well as being so depressed, that to me there was really nothing to look forward to.

I let him slip right through my fingers. He wrote, and so did I, but I really wasn't trying to make an impression on anyone. My thinking at the time was mainly, *who would want me if they knew what I had done?*

One person saw more potential in me than I did in myself: Art Levine from New York City was a frat brother of Annie's brother.

Art had come for a summer visit with Vance, and several times we all piled into Vance's new Chrysler convertible. Art took a liking to me right away. I think my husky voice belied the fact that I was quaking inside, and instead, I came across as being pretty much my own person. At least, that's what Art said.

He also told me, "You shouldn't be fooling around with these hicks in town. Why don't you go to the city where you can meet someone who's more your match?" (Apparently, he had seen or heard about the lackadaisical Ward.) Too bad I didn't take his advice.

CHAPTER 54

AS AN EXAMPLE of the big difference in my self-evaluation, the year before, when I was happy and carefree, I was the worthy advisor of the local Order of the Rainbow for Girls, a subsidiary of the Masons and Eastern Star. I was to preside at an initiation for a young novice who was only 13, and who had just entered the eighth grade. Thirteen was the age limit for new members. While the Masonic Order taught the same tenants of good and bad as it does today, the fact that it was very racially prejudiced didn't bother us.

In preparation for the formal initiation, I had to memorize six pages of single-line print in the Rainbow manual to lead the young girl through the stations. I did my job well and on the night of the initiation, felt confident, and I enjoyed escorting this little girl through what we hoped would lead to an admirable, conscientious adulthood.

I remember looking down at her when I talked to her, delivering my instructions as sincerely as I knew how. Somehow, I felt that she and I were the only ones in the room, and I knew what I said to her made a deep impression.

While I knew the State Advisor of the Rainbow Order was in the audience that night, I wasn't concerned with her presence and did my job as best I could. After the initiation, the state officer was asked for comments, and she said, "This has been an extraordinary evening. The worthy advisor delivered her part letter-perfect, and this is the first time, to my knowledge, an officer of that position has done so."

I was quite pleased but not surprised. I knew I had a good memory, although I didn't think it was that good. It was as though I was just reading the print from the book.

The point is that a year later when I stepped down as worthy advisor and Billie, who was just an office behind me, advanced to the head position, I did very poorly.

This was while I was in the throes of my guilt-complex when I knew I was doing everything wrong. I had to introduce my parents to the assembly, then conduct Billie to the head station, and it was as though I was still that eighth grader of long ago who couldn't perform in the drum corps. I did it all wrong. I stumbled through my speeches and was ineffective. I felt sure it was noted and no doubt the officials and other members wondered what was wrong with me.

I knew what was wrong but couldn't help it: I was going through another of my "habit" crises, and my entire world was topsy-turvy. There was no help for me except the nerve medicine I was taking. Also, as head of a group supposed to represent goodness and admiration for young women, I felt hypocritical. If the group had known what I had done, they would never have touted me as an example for young women.

CHAPTER 55

PROBABLY it was a coincidence, but Billie, Annie and I had to have extensive cosmetic dental work.

I had chipped the inside corner of my right front tooth in a fall when I was 10 years old and always felt self-conscious about it. So, I wanted it fixed. Billie had also chipped her front teeth when she hit a clothes line running full force. Annie had two small teeth on either side of her front teeth which had to be replaced.

We had all been advised by our hometown dentist that there was an excellent dentist in Kansas City who specialized in making partials to replace damaged or unhealthy teeth. The three of us made plans to see Dr. Crain and, while we were at it, to have a fling in Kansas City. Working for the newspaper allowed us the perk of a due bill at one of the larger, nicer hotels in the city where we could stay up to a week rent-free.

I told Bill Annis we were coming to the city and would be staying at the Mayo Hotel.

Bill wrote back, "I'm delighted and will make some plans."

We went to Kansas City by bus since none of us had a car but were able to go from the hotel to the dentist's office by city bus or taxi, which were quite inexpensive in those days.

For my first evening in the city, Bill picked me up at the hotel and we went to a movie with another couple, friends of Bill's who were unmarried. The young lady was quite sophisticated in a black linen dress which I considered much more appropriate than my cotton summer dress. But in my mental state at that time, very little that I did do seemed right for me. Somehow, I managed not to be a complete klutz, but I did feel very uncomfortable.

The next day, after our appointments with Dr. Crain, to get our teeth "fixed," I readied myself for dinner with Bill at one of Kansas City's best restaurants which was supposed to be a real night on the town. I did better at dressing for that occasion wearing a two-piece white bird's-eye pique skirt and jacket with a white lace peplum. I had designed it, and Mother had made it.

Bill and I went to the restaurant, which also had a small combo and dance floor, and I was enjoying our candlelight dinner. This was very much a grown-up thing for me to do, and something I hadn't done before especially with the countrified Ward.

I was forgetting my troubles over a glass of wine when who should walk in but Billie and Annie, both of them quite drunk. To make matters worse, and since they knew they couldn't get in the fancy place without an escort, they'd brought their taxi driver as a chaperone.

As always, I over-reacted and made the situation 10 times worse than it was. Bill asked me, "Is something bothering you?"

I had to be truthful and said, "That's my sister and good friend who just came in with that taxi driver." I couldn't disguise the fact that I was embarrassed but tried to face the situation as gracefully as I could.

In reality, it was funny, but I wasn't able to laugh about it for years. I think Bill enjoyed the whole scene, not maliciously, but he could see the humor.

Of course, once Billie and Annie saw me there with Bill, they left so as not to humiliate me further. I thought they had ruined my entire life. As "Miss Perfect of 1948," which Billie and Annie often called me, I was deeply upset.

The rest of the visit went well, and I enjoyed being with Bill, but in my depressed frame of mind, I didn't see him as being part of my future. In fact, I didn't see a future for me at all.

CHAPTER 56

WARD TOOK ALL of my various boyfriends quite well; he didn't look toward the future either. He was very happy to live with his mother, let her run the farm, have his dates with me, and see his buddies often for a beer. He did, however, keep pushing me for sex.

I became more and more depressed and even began hallucinating. For instance, when I saw a movie about a woman who had committed a murder, the question arose in my mind, *have I ever murdered anyone?* While I knew very well that I hadn't, the sick side of me wasn't so sure. I don't know who I thought I might have killed, but it was an obsession that stayed with me for several days.

Being around Richard at the office was difficult. Much the same as when I was a child in junior high school, when I tried to keep my distance from my male teachers, I tried not to get any closer to Richard than I had to. Since we were no longer involved in our little tawdry affair, I don't think Richard noticed how I avoided him. He, like everyone else, didn't know I was so greatly upset.

As a child, when the worries would overtake me, I had learned how to hide them and had never told anyone about my doubts and fears. I was good at hiding them. Mainly, while I thought I was crazy, I didn't want anyone else to think the same because what else could they do for me except send me to the state hospital?

In our little corner of the state, there were no psychiatrists. In fact, psychiatry hadn't been extensively explored and offered for the perusal of the general public.

It was just beginning to make in-roads even in the movies, such as the Ingrid Bergman-Gregory Peck film, *Spellbound*. Of course, Ingrid cured Gregory of his craziness in a matter of hours after he remembered that his brother's death had been caused by him becoming impaled on an iron trellis. I was afraid my condition couldn't be fixed that easily.

I think people with my obsessive inclination unless they have overt symptoms such as blowing on their hands or arms to do away with the demon thoughts, learn very well how to hide their illness. I could be in the throes of a deep depression and, if the phone rang or someone came to see me unexpectedly, could immediately change my mood and put on a convincing show of normalcy.

Once, much later, I was with an associate, (i.e., man), and was quite angry and crying when my mother called on the phone. I immediately stopped crying and put on a cheerful demeanor since I definitely didn't want her to know I was troubled.

The guy was dumbfounded and said, "Why, you're just a liar. You weren't crying at all; those were just crocodile tears to upset me."

I tried but could not convince him that they were real and that my distress at that time was genuine. Perhaps I had learned "method acting" without even knowing it.

CHAPTER 57

While my visit to Kansas City with Bill distressed me a great deal, he seemed to be even more charmed by me. The three of us had to go back to our dentist for further fittings that summer, but Bill was out of town. However, in the fall, after numerous hints from Bill, I invited him to Mooresville to spend the weekend with my family and me.

Since our house was small and we had no guest room, Annie's mother invited Bill to spend an overnight with them in their large Tudor house.

My dad bought a new hi-fi radio/phonograph in a handsome cabinet. My mother planned a steak dinner at our house for Annie, her brother, Ben, Billie and her fiancé, J.W., Bill and me, and my parents.

We had also made plans to go to nearby Springfield to one of the better nightclubs. Daddy and Mother enjoyed dinner, and while they were always charming to Billie's and my friends, they seemed to overwhelm Bill.

Merrily off we went. There wasn't much drinking; none

of us were heavy drinkers, and while my parents later became teetotalers, they quaffed a few that night. This was unfortunate, especially in my mother's case.

She had always been jealous of my father and, in her mind, she thought he paid too much attention to Annie. She was livid and didn't really make a scene, but it wasn't lost on any of us that she thought Daddy had played up to Annie.

I was embarrassed and angry. I felt they should have been on their dignity with this nice young man whom I was trying to impress rather than let their basic, rude instincts show—especially my mother's anger directed at my best friend!

The drive back home from Springfield was tense, to say the least, and Bill and I parted at my house with him going to Annie's home to spend the night with her family. He picked me up the next morning for breakfast and then he and I left for the day to drive down through the mountainous area south of Mooresville, and to have lunch.

To put it mildly, I wasn't happy. I was embarrassed about my parents' juvenile behavior, and still sad about my crisis. Bill, of course, noticed and tried to pry me out of my downcast mood. I'm sure he thought the entire incident was just trivial and in no way did it diminish his opinion of me, which was very high, I learned.

Bill said, "You know, I really like you. I'm sorry you're so sad, and I'd like to buy you a token of my affection for you."

I said, "I think you do like me and I like you, but I'm not in a very good mood today." "Pensive" would have explained it better, but that wasn't in my vocabulary. So, we went to a jewelry store, and all I chose was a small opaque stone heart on a neck chain. (I still have it.)

Actually, my self-worth was suffering so that I didn't think I deserved anything better. Bill apparently did since he said, "I'd really like to buy you something nicer." But I insisted that was all I wanted.

I managed to get through the day and did become more cheerful, but Bill took my unenthusiastic demeanor as a signal that I was not enjoying his company. That wasn't it at all; I liked him, but I was so disturbed that any thought of the future upset me.

A popular song of the day included the lyrics, "you were only fooling while I was falling in love." When the melody played on the car radio, Bill said, "That's the way I feel. But I'm afraid I'm the only one who feels anything."

I tried to assure him that wasn't the case at all, that I was just upset. I'm sure he didn't realize how upset I was. I wanted so much to be chaste and worthy of this nice young man's opinion of me, but that wasn't how I felt about myself at all.

However, I had another appointment with the dentist in Kansas City in about three weeks, so we made plans to see each other then. He sympathized, "I hope you feel better then." So did I but I didn't feel much hope at that juncture.

CHAPTER 58

BILL LEFT THAT EVENING, and the next day I was glad to get back to comfortable old Ward, whom I didn't need to impress. Ward was too laid-back to care a lot, anyway. He still thought he deserved to have sex, but he didn't make a big thing of it.

I think one of the reasons I continued seeing Ward was that he was easy-going. Also, I compared him with my dad who had always upset me with his temper outbursts.

Ward certainly didn't act that way—he seldom became angry. He seldom even became excited. I guess I came to the conclusion that life with him would be peaceful—not the clamoring, fighting, and arguing that I had grown up witnessing between my own parents, much of which I blamed for my then present unhappy state of mind. I knew enough about psychology to determine that I felt insecure, which resulted in being unsure of myself.

This resulted in not knowing what had happened that August 15, and the knowledge that I was, in fact, mentally ill. I knew what I was going through was not normal. I thought: *if I ever get married, I certainly won't fight in front of my kids. I'll get a divorce first.*

When I went back to Kansas City for my last dental appointment, I was more morose than ever. It didn't help that I was reading a depressing book about lepers in a Louisiana colony. It also didn't help that I went alone and stayed in my hotel room alone, except for the time I spent with Bill and his mother.

Another minor matter added to my depression. In addition to his profession as a fund-raiser, Bill was an excellent photographer. In looking at one of his albums, I ran across an odd photo of a man lying on his stomach with a horror-stricken look on his face.

I asked Bill, "What's wrong with that guy?"

He answered, "I wish you hadn't seen that. That man had just been run over by a train which cut him in half."

I'll remember that look of desperation and terror on his face for as long as I live.

This was early in November during the Truman-Dewey fight for the presidency. I remember hearing that Dewey had won, which didn't please me since, like many people who don't trust men with mustaches, I didn't like the upstart from New York. But that wasn't my major concern. The real problem was myself and my relationship with Bill. I knew I had to come to some kind of conclusion with him since he was not the type to take a courtship lightly.

One bright spot in the picture, however, was that my new partial was finished, which blended beautifully with my teeth. Now I had a nice smile, but as one of the worriers of the world, I was almost afraid to eat with it, that it would break off. But it didn't and improved my looks a good bit.

On my last day in Kansas City, I thought I should say something definite about our relationship. I told Bill, "I think it's best if we don't pursue our romance right now. It's not that I don't have feelings for you, but I have problems that need to be worked out before I'm ready to pursue any kind of relationship."

He replied, "Is there someone else, or am I just not the one?"

"There's no one definitely involved. I just need time to think things through."

We left it at that, although deep down I did feel I could depend on Ward for comfort and a relationship that didn't require a great deal of giving. That was certainly true: With Ward, there was very little effort involved. At that time, that was all I could handle.

After my return home, I only heard from Bill once more, at Christmas. That was just a card and note which stated, "I wish you well in whatever direction your life takes you. If it includes me, please let me know."

CHAPTER 59

RIGHT BEFORE THE HOLIDAYS, I realized I was becoming more and more nervous and depressed, and my thinking was greatly confused. I even began thinking about Marta, and it dawned on me that she was a lesbian. I also wondered if I might have those tendencies, too.

I was weighted down with guilt, so I took this quite seriously. Almost any aspect of sex upset me a great deal, and I worried excessively about it. I was also angry with my parents for not having told me the truth about Marta instead of just demanding I not see her without any explanation. Perhaps the truth would have absolved me of the guilt I felt.

During all this time it should be noted that Billie met, fell in love with, and married a nice young man, J.W., from Carterville. All of this went by me with as little involvement on my part as possible. I was her maid of honor but left the choice of a dress up to her.

Billie was lovely in a winter white tissue wool dress that she designed, and Mother made. I wore a pearl gray tissue wool dress. I scarcely remember her bridal shower, wedding, or reception. I just did what I was told. Otherwise, I was completely out of it.

Billie moved with J.W. to a small three-room house in Carterville where they were happy as larks. J.W. worked for his father who was a stone mason and owned a monument business. They were quite poor but very much in love, a love I'm happy to state that lasted throughout the years until both of them died.

Their marriage was not impeded by Billie's exposure to a dysfunctional family example forced upon us by our two endearing but immature parents. In fact, Billie told me many years later, that she was determined never to yell at her husband or create the scenes that she and I had to witness as we were growing up. Also, she was determined she would never expose her children to familial fighting.

I, on the other hand, was determined never to fight in front of my children, but my method of prevention was just to get a divorce. Both of us had formed our mindsets early in life, whether good or bad. The one factor that helped throughout most of it was that we maintained a sense of humor, especially where each other was involved. A good sense of humor is a buoying factor when the going gets rough.

Also, early in their marriage, Billie and J.W. happily announced that she was pregnant. We were all delighted. We knew Billie, with her sunny disposition and her love for "my J.W.," would get through whatever came their way, poverty or not. She was only 19, but she had matured quite rapidly. What I didn't know—and something she told me years later—was that she could have gotten a scholarship at the state university and her life would have been quite different.

"A mind is a terrible thing to waste" we were told later. That's true, although, without much formal education, Billie did do well in her later years. But that's her story. As someone else said, "There's a story in all of us."

CHAPTER 60

AFTER BILLIE'S MARRIAGE and move to Carterville, I was lonelier than ever and definitely more depressed. While I could not have confided in my sister about my real issue, at least she was a great deal of company and comfort for me.

I had finished junior college the preceding spring and graduated with honors. Somehow, in spite of my mental problems and obsessions, I had kept my grades up and graduated second in my class. I had all but a few girlfriends, having quit going to the sewing get-togethers and I had even missed a couple of sleepovers. I just wasn't interested in the girls anymore; I was too concerned with myself.

I continued with my uneventful courtship with Ward as well as my preponderance of just how bad a person I really was. I was mainly afraid that I wasn't a virgin any longer. Finally, I thought I would have to do something, so one cold, wet December evening after work I went to our family doctor, Dr. North. He said, "What seems to be wrong with you, young lady?"

I told him, "I've been very nervous lately and have something on my mind which I'm trying to settle since I don't really know for sure what happened. It happened on the day the war ended."

I haltingly told him about the possible rape, though I didn't consider it to be that at all. I actually thought it was my fault for having an affair with a married man. I was feeling guilty, as I've read most rape victims do.

When I completed my tale, I asked him, "Do you know what I mean when I say I don't know what actually happened?"

He then made a big mistake: He put his knees on either side of my knees and held my hands, and said, "No, I don't know what you mean, but I think you're just nervous. I'm going to give you some nerve medication which will help you sleep better, and maybe you can get through this."

I was horrified; the last thing I wanted was closeness or intimacy with an older man, and I was greatly frightened and affronted by his action. I'm sure he only looked at me as the same little girl he had vaccinated or treated for a cold through the years.

He knew nothing about psychiatry, I'm sure, or if he had any dealings with it at all, he probably thought it was a lot of nonsense. A lot of doctors did in those days.

CHAPTER 61

DR. NORTH didn't have the slightest notion about what I was trying to tell him. Had I used the word "rape" he might have understood, but that wasn't in my vocabulary. I simply attempted to describe what happened between Richard and me that day and that I didn't know exactly what it was.

But Christmas was coming on, and even though it was my favorite holiday, I couldn't get too involved. Then I discovered the elixir of life—booze! I was beginning to learn that alcohol would assuage my troubled mind somewhat and I could forget that I was such a despicable person.

I remember that Christmas in a haze since I was drunk most of the time. Although I was only 20, I was served drinks when Ward took me out and, while he didn't over-do, he didn't seem to mind that I did. (He probably thought that was one way to get me to go to bed with him—the pursuit of all his dreams.)

I held my liquor pretty well and don't remember any-one being concerned about my drinking, except probably me. Having the religious upbringing that I did, it naturally weighed on my conscience that I shouldn't be drinking all that stuff, but since everything else in my life was haywire, I didn't let it bother me. At least, I could forget some of the things I didn't want to think about.

After the holidays, the usual doldrums set in and I was once again faced with reality. The worst scenario for me at that time was being around Richard at the newspaper. Fortunately, he wasn't on my case; but I'm sure there was some other hapless employee feeling his wrath. He wasn't happy unless he was persecuting someone.

But finally, I could take no more. I knew I had to talk to someone, so I made an appointment with one of the best-thought-of doctors in town, Dr. Dudley. I was so up-set I could hardly tell him what was wrong. Beyond tears by then, I did manage to tell him there was something in life that I didn't understand, didn't really know how to talk about, and that it was important for me to get it straight-ened out.

It was also very important that he understand what I was talking about. Much to my relief, he said, "I think I know what you're talking about. There are just some things that we don't really know or aren't sure of."

But knowing I was greatly distraught and that a 15-min-ute session wasn't going to do much for me, he suggested I come back to his office that evening to tell him the whole story.

I'm quite sure Dr. Dudley had my best interests in mind, and, at the time, since I didn't even own a car, going to the nearby city to see a psychiatrist was out of the question. He did the next best thing; he played psychiatrist himself.

I don't regret that he did, even though I needed more expert treatment at the time. I just desperately needed someone to talk to, and he was a rescuer. I totally appreciate what he did and have no regrets. If my life hadn't taken the course that it did then, I don't know what would have happened to me.

I told him as best I could about Richard and my "affair" with him. In a small town, no doubt Dr. Dudley and Richard crossed paths socially, and I'm sure Dr. Dudley was a little titillated to learn of Richard's indiscretions. Of course, he wouldn't have told anyone, or so I assumed, so I gave him the entire truth.

He listened carefully and commiserated with me, then said, "What you really want to know is whether or not you've ever had intercourse."

I answered, "I had hoped to be a virgin when I married, and the fact that I don't know troubles me."

I wasn't surprised when he said, "You have a boyfriend, don't you? Well, go ahead and have sex with him, and that way you'll know. But be sure to be careful."

Famous last words.

I was given a prescription to calm my nerves, as well as the verbal prescription, so out I went and did what Dr. Dudley had told me to do.

Ward and I first had sex in the front seat of his car, which was nice enough for someone like me who didn't expect much of the amenities of life, but I wasn't very comfortable. I would say the assignation was pleasant, but I still didn't know about Richard. Which meant nothing was resolved.

At my next appointment with Dr. Dudley, I told him I hadn't allayed the worries I had about Richard and sex, and he said that an automobile was no place to have sex. "Why doesn't your boyfriend take you to a nice comfortable motel?" I told Ward about this, and so he did.

But working around Richard at the newspaper became no easier, and I longed for a day where I felt good about myself and my world, where I didn't have to face the vagaries of what I perceived to be a grownup existence.

I told my parents: "You know I haven't been feeling well lately and think it's time I quit my job. I want to stay at home for a while and relax since the work is becoming too much for me."

Of course, they didn't suspect the real reason—Richard—and maybe I obliterated that also in my mind. I simply thought staying at home with my parents would help my mental outlook a great deal.

When I told Richard I was quitting, it might not have come as too much of a surprise for him. He had noticed that I wasn't at all cheerful, having lost any enthusiasm I had ever had for the job.

He was certain that something was wrong with me, so he asked, "Are you mad at any of us?"

I answered, "No, I just find it hard to go on here."

"Is it because of me?"

"Well, yes, it is. I feel very guilty about what happened between us a few years ago. It's something I can't seem to forgive myself for. I don't blame you entirely, but I'm bothered about what really happened that day, you know... that day."

Richard was more understanding than I thought he would be. He had always been such a selfish creature; I didn't think he ever gave anyone else a thought. Apparently, he did. At least he asked, "What about it aren't you sure?"

"Did we really have intercourse?" I asked.

"No, we didn't. I tried, but we didn't."

One would think that would have appeased me, but I was so drenched in guilt it was going to take more than that to cure my sick little mind. The situation had gone too far to be immediately reversible.

I don't know when, or if, Richard knew I had seen Dr. Dudley, and aired all my dirty linen before him. If he did know, he had reason to feel a little indignant, with his former lover telling all to a social component on his own level. I'm sure seducing a teenager wasn't something a distinguished professional wanted bandied about town. It reeks of child molestation.

Had Richard ever asked for advice—or questioned his actions when it came to his romantic involvements—he might well have considered the age of his partner; also, the stability of her mind. If you're going to pick someone out for a love affair, make sure she's sound of mind. I wasn't. Richard could well have rued the day he thought about any flirtation with me.

CHAPTER 62

MOTHER AND DADDY didn't question my decision to resign or bring up the pertinent question about what I was going to do with the rest of my life. They knew I had a small amount of money saved, and my expenses at home were as they had always been: I was still their daughter and so deserved to live with them as long as I was moral and above-board.

I was willing to become a spinster. All I wanted was peace and quiet, no Richard, no stress, no guilt feelings. I thought that the sanctuary of my childhood home would provide that.

I was wrong.

The first week of my new retirement, I slept late, which I had always liked to do, helped with the washing and ironing; helped with the cooking, and even consented to dust the furniture. I was fairly happy in my cocoon of oblivion to all else around me. I had no future, as far as I knew then, and didn't want one. I liked helping keep house, and I began to think I was merely a frustrated housekeeper.

I continued to see Ward. Why not? He put no pressure or stress on me to do anything, not even having sex now that he had discovered I would do it. Of course, I don't think he would rate me a "10" on a scale of 1 to 10 for originality, lust or even affection. From what I remember, our love-making was as mundane as our everyday lives. It was all I could handle at the time.

Or so I thought.

The next week I missed my period.

Since I was always pretty regular, I was for once in my life able to face facts without panicking. I knew something was wrong, especially when I didn't feel well a morning or so later. I didn't have morning sickness but didn't feel right.

A couple of nights later when I went to the movies with Ward, and then later to our secret trysting spot, I took the bull by the horns and asked Ward, "Are you planning to marry me eventually?"

He didn't seem too surprised by this and answered, "Yeah, I guess I was."

"Well, you might as well do it soon because I think I'm pregnant. Even if you are intending to eventually, I think it would be best to get married now and then if I'm not pregnant, it won't matter because I think I want to marry you anyway."

Ward thought this over only for about 30 seconds, then said, "I guess you're right. We really should get married. When do you want to do it?"

From all the movies I'd seen, and that we had seen together, you would have thought we could have had a more dramatic proposal than that. It's a good thing I wasn't a romantic young thing who expected her proposal to be the high point of her life. Our engagement was more like a business arrangement, except we were both as poor as church mice and certainly had nothing to offer to bargain with. Nor even clever repartee.

CHAPTER 63

BOY, one week I was a spinster out of a job. The next I was a mother-to-be. The week after that I was betrothed. We Midwesterners don't waste much time making up our minds.

Since we knew everyone would speculate about the reason we were getting married so suddenly, Ward and I decided we didn't want any more notoriety than necessary, so we made plans to have a simple ceremony at his Presbyterian church with our good friends, Jim and Mary, as attendants.

With the following Saturday as the wedding date, it didn't take me long to determine that there was no reason to buy myself an expensive dress that I obviously wouldn't be wearing for the next nine months. Practical as I was, I also knew we needed whatever money that new dress would have cost.

Since everything seemed to be falling into place, it was no surprise to me that my mother conveniently went into the hospital the Monday before the designated day of the wedding. I had all week, at home by myself, with Daddy also away at work, so I decided to fix up Billie's pretty white tissue wool dress in my own style for a wedding dress.

Her original gown had a draped collar forming a wide neckline which didn't suit my more pristine nature and personality, even being unmarried and pregnant notwithstanding.

I suppose Billie finally forgave me for cutting up her pretty cocktail-length dress, rather than ripping it, to add a high-neck, good-girl-yoke look. I did it all without a pattern and even took off the bustle in the back.

I liked the dress much better and thought I looked quite virgin-like when Ward and I spoke our vows the following Saturday night. Ward even surprised me and bought a new suit.

Of course, he couldn't afford an engagement ring but gave me a single white gold band with four small diamonds. It was quite pretty, and I was proud of it. In fact, the entire small marriage went off without a hitch. It was a joyous little affair in spite of the bride being at least three weeks pregnant. Compared to today's statistics, I practically was a virgin. But since there is no degree of pregnancy, either you are, or you aren't, it was a good thing that dress was off-white.

CHAPTER 64

WARD AND I didn't intend to tell our parents we had married until the following week, mainly because my mother was still hospitalized, and we thought she would take it better later. Both my parents were delighted and wished us well, but Ward's widowed mother, Edith, wasn't too happy. Ward was her baby and helper on the farm. Also, we announced without even asking first that we planned to make our home with her. I doubt that too many women would have taken that news gracefully.

Ward and I had already talked over our arrangements and, while we would be living under the same roof, we would be in separate parts of the house, which was quite large.

Our abode would include the entire upstairs which was one large room with dormer windows on all four sides. The two on opposite walls overlooked the yard and were quite pretty bay windows with box seats underneath.

I could see many possibilities for the upstairs which had a stairway leading into a small back room of the house which was to be our kitchen. It also had a door leading to an outside screened-in porch.

Although there was no running water in the room, it was just off the bathroom, so I saw no problem in getting my water there. Also, there was no refrigerator, but we deduced that we could use Edith's which was in her kitchen just outside the west door of our small makeshift kitchen.

Next on the agenda was a cook stove, so our first purchase was a propane gas-fueled Maytag which we bought the first week after our announcement. Considering how poor we were, one would think we might have purchased a cheaper one, but Ward was a friend of the Maytag dealer.

I don't know what Edith thought about this new young woman, full of plans, sweeping into her home, but, I will say, she was very nice about it. Perhaps I was so full of myself during that period; I didn't notice that she might be unhappy. But she certainly didn't complain.

To go back a bit, though, after we announced that we were now Mr. and Mrs., we took a weekend honeymoon trip to nearby Arkansas. This was when I really began to notice some of the discomforts of being pregnant.

Ward smoked a pipe and, while heretofore I had always liked the smell of his tobacco, on the way to our honeymoon suite, when he lit up his pipe, I became quite ill. I didn't vomit, but I had to open the window of the car for some fresh air, or I would have. Since Ward wasn't about to quit smoking, I eventually became accustomed to the smell but still remember it.

I noticed another disadvantage of pregnancy—I could barely eat. We stopped at a well-known fish house for fried trout, which was one of my favorite delicacies, but I couldn't even eat that. So, I was a cheap date for the weekend, just mincing on my food.

But I was happy. I didn't mind that I was married and already expecting a baby. This was a new adventure for me, and I felt almost independent for probably the first time in my life. I didn't see Ward as an oppressor, and he wasn't, in fact. Ward was too laid-back to issue orders.

While this may not sound like the love affair of the century, we were in love. Neither of us was loquacious when it came to expressing our feelings, but I don't think either of us felt we had been duped or gotten into an arrangement, not to our liking.

CHAPTER 65

WE SETTLED into blissful matrimony. Although we had very little income, only Ward's veteran's pay for attending farm school on Saturdays, we didn't seem to mind. We needed many things but, as was the custom in our small-town society, we were given a nice shower. We received much of what we would need to set up housekeeping.

My favorite gift was an expensive Better Homes and Gardens Cook Book which had all the basics as well as more complicated cookery. I read it like a novel and, while I could hardly boil water before we were married, I emerged as a pretty good cook. That was my passion. I would rather cook than eat.

There's truth in that statement. As my pregnancy became more developed, I found there was very little that I could eat, and even a smaller amount that I could keep down. I'm sure Edith noticed right away that I threw up each morning, whether I had eaten much the night before or not. She didn't take her meals with us, but she was a wise old bird.

Our living quarters were less than luxurious but adequate, although very sparse. We were undaunted because we were young, especially since we had grown up during the Depression and had learned how to make-do.

I kept a bucket of water on a small stand, and our table served not only as a counter for preparing food but also as a place for meals.

And a real perk—we had a small screened-in porch outside our kitchen. Where the table and chairs came from, I don't know, but they enabled us to have pleasant summer meals on our porch.

As soon as we were settled and got into the swing of things, such as being married, the doldrums miraculously began to leave me. I was swept up in my new roles as wife and expectant mother, and the ghosts of the past, including Richard and all the guilt that went with him, settled into the back of my mind.

I didn't experience the old qualms of self-doubt and uncertainties concerning all the mundane things I did each day. Probably the fact that Ward was approving of me gave me some of the confidence I lacked. Also, I had someone other than myself to think about, and I was quite anxious to please my new husband—especially when I cooked for him. Some of the dishes turned out ghastly, but he was game and ate them anyway.

Ward's large family took to me quite readily, including his two married sisters who lived nearby—Janie and Dorothy. I was soon to learn the family was quite penurious but, since Ward and I had no money to squander anyway, they couldn't criticize us for that. I was beginning to notice differences between his family and mine, but I didn't let them bother me. Instead, I became quite fond of all of them.

We also had a fairly brisk social life. We still conferred with Jimmy and Mary, our wedding attendants, and Ward's friend, Eugene Moriondo, or "Moe" as Ward called him, who was also a farming partner of sorts. Moe and his homely wife, Eloise, invited us over quite a bit.

Eloise was big-busted and had a nice figure, but she was certainly no beauty while Moe was quite handsome in his dark Italian way. I could see right away that Eloise was a baby-machine; they already had two small boys, born about 18 months apart, and another baby was on the way.

But Eloise didn't mind. She was plainly enamored of her handsome husband. Moe had had many girlfriends, Ward said, but he had met Eloise in Texas during the war when he was stationed near her home-town of Galveston.

Ward said, in explaining Eloise's charm for Moe, "She was quite a business-woman, and owns several apartment buildings in Texas." He also alluded to the fact that perhaps that was one of her charms for Moe, "that, and her busty figure."

Maybe so, but she was nice, too.

CHAPTER 66

FOR THE FIRST TIME in my 21 years, I felt I had a purpose and was doing things well. My qualms about making mistakes disappeared with my new self-confidence and interests in homemaking. I surmised that this was what I had been leading up to all my life, having my own domain, small though it was, and someone to do things for—Ward, in this case.

Then there was the baby on the way, and once I began to feel a little better, after the first month, or so of morning sickness, I looked forward with affection for the little tyke, never doubting that I would do a good job with him... or her.

I was chirpier; I was happier, and I began to plan for a future that had eluded me the previous year and a half when I had been in the throes of my guilt obsession. My "habit" at that time didn't seem to exist; I spent very little time worrying about the small concerns. But, I was still neurotic and set in my ways. Just because I had said "I do" it wasn't a cure-all for my problems.

But for a while I had fun. Being energetic and always a do-it-yourselfer, I made a pretty cover of red, green, pink and yellow plaid, combined with yellow linen-like fabric, for a daybed that Mother and Daddy had given us. I also made pillows with piping, even though I had never done anything like that before. But Mother showed me how.

One of the bay windows had a window seat, so I made a cover for the cushion, and the other bay window contained a round pedestal Victorian-style table which Ward, and I painted white. It was to be our "dining" table if we ever had guests. With the addition of chairs, a rocker and miscellaneous items from both our families, we managed to furnish most of our upstairs apartment.

The nicest area, however, was the space where we put our bed. My parents had given us a new Hollywood-type bed with a pretty mahogany headboard as one of our wedding gifts, and Edith loaned us a walnut chest of drawers which matched fairly well.

In addition to this splendor, Edith had loaned us the use of a pretty, but old-fashioned, dressing table, the type with swing-away mirrors on either side. It fit right into the center of the dormer in our bedroom area.

Since we didn't have a closet, I suggested to Ward that my grandfather could build cubbies on either side of the dressing table and we could have individual closets, one for him and one for me. I reasoned they wouldn't have doors, but we could worry about that later.

All he needed to do was build the forms and cover the area with plasterboard which I was sure cost a mere pittance. Since we didn't have any money anyway, why worry about it. I knew we'd get it someplace.

Ward didn't seem worried either, so I gleefully told him, "We can paint all the walls in the upstairs light blue with the exception of the bedroom area, which we can paper in a pretty blue floral print."

"That's fine with me," Ward said. "But who are you going to get to do the wallpapering?"

"That's easy," I told him. "My Aunt Goldie does it for her church, and she's very cheap." So, Mother's older half-sister actually did the paper and charged us a pittance, which was all we could afford.

I was full of ideas, and, miraculously, they all worked. Grandpa did build our closets, we papered and painted, and the place began to look lovely and very homey.

I also got better acquainted with my grandfather. By that time, I was driving Ward's new car every day, and considered it my own. I picked up Grandpa each morning to do the work since he didn't own a car. We talked a lot, and I learned he was smarter than I had thought.

One day we were going across the railroad tracks, and Grandpa sagely told me, "If you go 'annie-goglin,' it won't be so bumpy." I had never heard that phase before and surmised it was something he brought up from Louisiana when he relocated to our area while a young man. I've never heard the phase again or seen it in print, so am somewhat at a loss as to how to spell it, but it seems to be similar in definition to "cattywampus." Meaning, you would cross the tracks diagonally to reduce the severity of the bumps.

Of course, there was the question of the floors which were bare and had never been varnished, so I bestowed on Ward the responsibility of getting them sanded down and polished. With his brother's, Charles, help, and that of my dad and the two brothers-in-law, we accomplished that also.

We were set. Or so I thought.

In spite of my persona of optimism, and carefree, cavalier attitude, there were bound to be some demons left in me. I'm sorry to say there were and, before too long, they came out of their hiding place.

CHAPTER 67

WHILE THIS may not sound like the love-match of the century, Ward and I did love each other; I think we were both happy in our new-found marital state.

But, sad to say, we argued, probably just like every other young couple. Although, for me, it was a crisis, as any type of contention was. I shall be honest and admit I started it—or at least precipitated it.

One day, Ward made a remark about the new baby on the way, and I took it as a signal that he wasn't especially happy that we were soon to be a threesome.

I accusingly said, "You didn't really want the baby, did you?"

Ward, in his oft-tactless manner, and lack of knowing how to treat an over-sensitive pregnant female, said, "Well, I would rather have waited 'til we were more on our feet."

This was just what the meanness in me was looking for. I got all puffed up and nose out of joint, made a big issue of the fact that he "didn't want to marry me after all, and that he didn't even want our baby."

Of course, that's not what he said or meant, but it assuaged my immature proclivity for starting trouble and imagining the worst.

However, it was not my nature to pout long, so even though we went to bed that night without making up, by the next day I was over the "insult," and we got on with our lives.

Pregnant though I was, I was a strong girl, and hard work didn't bother me. Edith even complimented me that "Jackie's not lazy and always has a project going."

Yes, I did, but I wish now the compliment had been about my "sweet disposition and kindness to others." I can see that as perfect as I thought I was, I was a woefully maladjusted, bitter person. I had a lot of growing up to do.

And even though my life was greatly improved in my new role as wife and mother-to-be, things weren't altogether a bed of roses. We had finished most of the work on our apartment and were quite proud of it. But with the summer came the farm work—or what there was of it.

I soon realized that Ward and his mother weren't full-scale farmers and weren't going to make a pile of money out of their operations. Most of the income was from the sale of cattle, poultry, and eggs. Apparently, in the fall, there would be a harvest of hay or grain for animal consumption.

Ward had a tractor and, in early spring, did the planting with the help of Moe; then he, in turn, helped Moe. But his income wasn't steady. In fact, as far as I could tell, his income was practically nil except for his $100 per month veterans' check, which was paid in return for his attending farming classes on Saturdays.

It didn't make me too happy to realize that Edith knew all our business and that any additional money Ward brought in came through her. She was the boss; Ward was her helper. This didn't seem the way a marriage ought to be. I thought the husband went to work each day, earned wages, and brought his check home to be disbursed between him and his wife.

Then another problem reared its ugly head. I discovered that Ward was lazy. He wouldn't get up in the mornings until he had to, or when his mother called him and told him it was time to go to work. If there was nothing pressing going on, he sometimes slept until noon.

I liked to sleep late myself, having never been an early riser, but this smacked of pure laziness and irresponsibility to me. With a baby on the way, I wondered about his priorities—if he even had any.

No, all was not happy in our household. I was worried about bills and how we were even going to pay the hospital bill when our baby came. But when I asked Ward about this, he said, "Don't worry. I have some money set aside, and if we need any more, Mom will help."

MOM!!! I didn't want any help from Mom. I didn't want Mom involved in our life or finances in any way. I was becoming disenchanted with playing house with Ward.

We quarreled. I wanted him to get a job like other young husbands. I wanted friends but should point out that Ward wasn't particularly interested in a social life. He would rather just sleep than make the effort to go out or plan anything for us, other than visits to his two sisters' homes.

Then the inevitable happened. The matter of Richard came up. I should have known it would, and I can't say that I wasn't partly to blame. In a moment of weakness and thinking it would help lift my guilt before we married, I had told him about Richard.

Big mistake.

Ward became angry in one of our arguments, and said, "I'm not even sure that baby you're carrying is mine."

I made things worse by saying, "I suppose you think Richard had something to do with it."

Fatal last words. He retorted, "I wouldn't be at all surprised."

I went home and spent the night with my parents, stating that we had had a bad argument. It was a silly, juvenile quarrel, and when Ward realized what he had said, he came to my parents' and told me, "I didn't mean what I said, and won't you please come home? I missed you and know our baby is mine."

Since that seemed the best solution to our problem, I went home to await the arrival of the baby, which was about two months away.

We settled back into our "playhouse" existence, but I was becoming increasingly aware that we were poor. I longed for Ward to get a job, so we would have a steady income and not be dependent upon his mother to dole out money when our $100 didn't last through the month.

Ward didn't seem to mind this fact at all. He was happy; he had never been financially solvent (neither had I, for that matter), but he didn't care. Not as long as he had a good car, of which he reluctantly, let me claim "owner-ship."

Once during a conversation with Mother and Billie, I said, "I'll come to get you in my car." Ward snorted and derisively said, "MY car? Where do you get off claiming the car? It's mine." I was not only embarrassed but stunned since I had always thought what belonged to one spouse belonged to the other. Not so, I was finding out.

He was insensitive in other little ways, too. Since I knew we had no money and I was still euphoric enough not to get in the habit of nagging, I made do with what I had. It was no problem for me to improvise a maternity top when the weather cooled in the fall.

Billie, who had already had her baby, a girl named Tory, gave me a black maternity skirt, so I scabbed from my pre-nuptial wardrobe a winter white wool jersey dress that had a yoke from which cascaded a gathered top and fairly full skirt drawn up at the waist.

I simply ripped off the bodice from the dress yoke and replaced it with the skirt, which I also gathered and buttoned down the front. The outfit was cute and amply roomy to cover my extending belly.

When I tried it on with the black skirt to show Ward, he said sarcastically, "Now, don't you think you're cute?"

I was appalled. Since the outfit hadn't cost him a cent, except for perhaps some buttons—and I had been inge-nious enough to make something from practically noth-ing—I thought it was crass of him to say such a thing. Also, even as young and unwise as I was, I knew that when a woman's pregnant, she feels liked a beached whale. Any little compliment goes a long way. In my mind, he was remiss in making fun of me.

This did NOT lead to a pleasant evening or ensuing days. That's when I first began to dislike my husband and when I started to wonder what I had gotten into. I'm sure I told my mother and, though she tried to downplay it, her dislike of Ward was becoming a fester for her, too.

In spite of the problems, I firmly believed that I was much better off mentally in my grown-up state of being wife and future mother. I was happy doing for my husband, although he wasn't too eloquent when it came to expressing appreciation. But I also knew that was Ward.

One of the qualities I liked about him when we were dating, was that he didn't make flowery speeches which would have embarrassed me. I could do without that poetry and mush. A little sincerity goes a long way, but I still felt the greatest lovers on the movie screen were a bunch of twits.

Our social life was not very active, except with our families. I had lost contact with most of the girls in my sewing group, as well as those with whom I attended junior college. I was guilty of neglect, and I wasn't proud that I had had to *get* married and was certain everyone knew and discussed the reasons why.

Also, I wasn't proud that I had married a farmer, especially one who was under his mother's thumb. I didn't feel we were our own little family—yet. But I had hopes. I guess hope was what kept me in a cheerful state.

Another problem cropped up, too. I noticed that Ward wasn't exactly the life of the party or host excellente when we were around people, other than his family. *Being a boy from the country, what did I expect?* I knew he was no great conversationalist, and his suave, silent manner was one of the things that drew me to him. Woefully, I was growing up; double woefully, he was not.

Then our baby boy, Todd arrived, and that ended our game of playing house. It was a difficult delivery since he weighed nine pounds, five ounces. I think I remember the pain but have read that if women could recall the extent of the agony, they would have no more children after the first one. I guess the intensity of the pain doesn't exactly register in our brains.

I do remember that as I was coming out of the anesthesia, I thought I heard the nurses or someone say, "It's a girl." I thought to myself, *Oh, no. Wardy will be disappointed.* Then I found out it was a boy and was very happy.

But when they brought that little boy to me, I didn't think he was pretty at all, with his round red face. He apparently didn't like my looks either because he took one look at me and began howling. Right away I thought, *this kid doesn't like me at all.* Of course, I was wrong, but my initial assessment should have been a warning to me that motherhood was not going to be easy.

All this time in our game of playing marriage, I haven't mentioned sex, so will do so now.

It was good.

CHAPTER 68

AFTER A WEEK's stay in the hospital, Todd and I were allowed to go home. Getting adjusted to the situation wasn't easy, even though Todd was a good-natured baby, contrary to what I was afraid of when I first saw him.

I breastfed him, and it seemed to be working, but I had lost my sense of euphoria, or happiness, and became sorely depressed. My old bugaboo of mental problems came back, and I couldn't understand why I wasn't more contented as a mother and wife.

Since it was winter, Ward did less and less farming and less and less work. He liked to hang around the house, and, while I was pleased he was so interested in the new baby, I worried what the future held for us, given Ward's seemingly cavalier attitude about work and providing.

One day as we were driving into town, I approached the subject of our future plans and what I could expect in the way of a secure financial picture. Ward blithely told me, "What's wrong with the way things are now? We have enough."

"Enough?" I said with alarm, "just what are we going to do about our future and how do we plan to educate Todd? Don't you want him to go to college?"

Ward amazed me when he said, "I think we're doing fine. I didn't go to college, and I'm happy. Why can't Todd be?"

"But," I countered, "don't you want to provide a few luxuries and a better way of life than just hand-to-mouth like we have now?"

He answered, "I don't want to work too hard and don't see any reason for it, especially since the government takes a big hunk out of every penny you make. I'd just as soon not make any money rather than have to give it away."

Hearing this was a blow as these were certainly not the answers I was expecting from a new father. I had always thought the manly thing to do was to want to provide the best they could for their family. That was the way my dad was, and I was stunned by this lackadaisical attitude.

Thus, ended paradise for me, or the fragments of what was left of it. Despair had been slowly encroaching throughout the last few months of pregnancy, and if I was feeling depressed before, hearing what Ward had to say put me over the brink.

I sunk lower into my depression and then into the Habit. I had thought trouble again and became unsure of myself, especially as it concerned my duties as a wife and mother. Fortunately, I had enough stability left to properly care for Todd, but the stilts had suddenly been pulled out from under me.

I returned to the way I was before I became pregnant, and I don't think it was all post-pregnancy depression.

I had to shoulder the full responsibility of rearing this new little baby since I had lost confidence in Ward and was dismayed at his attitude about being a father. Of course, he loved Todd, I was sure, but at 28 years of age, I thought he should be making concrete plans for our future.

In feeling this way again, I had no one to turn to except Dr. Duncan. At my first check-up for myself and Todd, after we were released from the hospital, I told him, "I'm afraid I'll become as dejected as I was last February when I first came to you."

He answered, "Well, Jackie, we know you were happy when you were pregnant, but we can't keep you pregnant all the time. You and your husband are going to have to work out your differences. I suspect living under the same roof with his mother is adding to your problems, but I don't know what to tell you to do about that."

Thanks a lot, Doc.

Shortly after that, and without any useful help from the Doc, I unleashed my despair upon the confines of our apartment, screaming my heart out. Then, I fled with Todd to my parents' house as I described in Chapter One.

SECTION THREE

SEARCHING FOR

Truth

CHAPTER 69

TODD AND I settled back in with Ward and Edith, and I determined to make new plans about our life.

At about this time, Billie and J.W. announced that they might be moving to Texas. J.W.'s father was a stone mason and owned a monument business in Carterville. But he was tired of the strains of running his own business and keeping records, although he was a success at it.

He had received a solid offer to sell the business and had previously been offered an excellent position as superintendent of a rock quarry in Texas. So, in selling the business, he was, in fact, forcing J.W. to seek other employment. Naturally, he hoped J.W., Billie and little Tory would go to Texas with him and the rest of the family.

If Ward could get a job there also, I felt it would be a way out of our trap and although the wages wouldn't be high, it at least, equaled independence from Ward's mother.

Billie said she would ask her father-in-law if he would hire Ward. J.W., and Sr. knew Ward to be a nice, presentable young man, and he knew I was a responsible person, so he said, "Sure, why not?"

But he asked us not to come down until he got settled into his new position and also until Billie and J.W. had made the move. This was an excellent idea since we were going into a vast no-man's-land about which we knew nothing.

J.W. Sr. and his family left for the little town of Mc-Cary, Texas, right after Christmas. I didn't have too much trouble convincing Ward we should go also since after I had left the farm with Todd, he realized he missed both of us and was willing to do anything to keep us together.

I didn't feel I was being unfair to Ward—to force him to take a job about which he knew nothing. After all, I wasn't standing in the way of his life-long dream to farm. If Ward had any dreams at all, it would have been to get by with as little work as possible, have a good time, and sleep until noon.

Off we went in January of 1950. Billie had written that she and J.W. were comfortably ensconced in a makeshift apartment in what had once been an army hospital close to the military base in McCary. After the war, it had been converted to apartments that were partially furnished. They were certainly not luxurious, but they were adequate. Every unit was different, depending on the arrangement of rooms in the original structure.

Billie, J.W., and Tory had one very large room which served as bedroom, living room and dining area. She also had a small kitchen off this room as well as a bathroom. Fortunately, all the apartments had private baths.

We fared better in that we had more room, but our five-room accommodation didn't have the warmth and charm that Billie's had. We had a kitchen, small dining room, two bedrooms connected by a hallway, and a large sparsely furnished living room. Nirvana it was not; home it was. But it was true independence, one of the criteria I had in making the move to a place 300 miles away.

We settled in, Ward started his job, and I tried to make our hospital-ward abode as homey as I could. Since we had filled the car with as much as possible and stored the rest of our belongings in Edith's barn, I didn't have a lot to work with. We certainly had no money since Ward worked for minimum wage, whatever that was back in those days.

However, I had overlooked and ignored for years to come—to my regret—the effect of our move on Mother and Daddy. In one fell swoop, they had lost both their daughters. I'm sure they were distraught and worried about me since it had become evident that I wasn't entirely wrapped too tightly.

It wasn't too surprising when Mother and Daddy showed up by train about three weeks after Ward and I had arrived in McCary. We were happy to see them, Billie, too, and fortunately, Ward and I had an extra bedroom with which to accommodate them.

My mother was her usual cheerful self, advising me how to make the best of my meager surroundings. She always looked on the bright side, a fact which I didn't come to appreciate until many years later.

I was too concerned about my own life to consider my parents' feelings. But perhaps I'm being a little hard on myself. I was very young—younger in maturity than my years. I also had a young child to care for, and I was discovering our new independence wasn't the cure-all of our problems, although it did help.

Then another situation arose which might have been the result of our move, the result of my unstable mental condition, or just the result of a bad, dysfunctional lifestyle. Todd began crying a lot, something he hadn't done up until that time.

I was still breastfeeding him, but as soon as he nursed and fell asleep, he immediately awakened. I spent many sleepless nights with him and didn't know how to console the poor child as he continued to cry. My parents were also concerned.

The situation became serious, not only for Todd but for myself, I realized, when one sleepless night I lost control and loudly yelled at my baby, "Shut up!" Then I actually whacked him on the bottom. While I might not have hurt him, I startled him, and he, of course, bawled even louder.

I knew something had to be done. I couldn't go on this way. Mother came in to help calm both the baby and me—and without recrimination.

The next morning, my parents urged me to take the baby to a doctor since his crying was much too urgent. We had been attending the Baptist Church, and the minister recommended a reliable physician in the small town to whom most of the parents took their children.

We went the next day and, right away, after I told the doctor I had been breastfeeding the baby, he obtained a sample of my milk. It, of course, was almost blue-white.

That's when he told me, "Through strain or for whatever reason, your milk is far short of satisfying the baby." He added, "Todd, at his age of about three months, is far below the standard progress of where he should be."

Immediately the doctor gave me a formula for Todd,

and we wasted no time in obtaining all the supplies. The result was most gratifying; Todd loved his new diet and slept soundly. The poor child was undernourished. Since then, I've never been a proponent of breastfeeding. Babies are much better off with a good, old-fashioned formula. Nervous mothers aren't meant to breastfeed.

CHAPTER 70

THE PROBLEM with Todd had been resolved, but there were others.

Ward didn't like his job, which was hard labor, so in retaliation for forcing him to move to Texas, he criticized me. My cooking wasn't good. I didn't properly attend to the baby, although he was becoming a fat, gurgling, happy child. So, my depression deepened.

One day, I read in the Waco paper that a mental health clinic (a new term to me at the time) had been set up at nearby Baylor University by the Psychology Department. It was free to the public; all you had to do was call and make an appointment.

I showed the item to Billie, and she thought it would be great for me. Ward, however, was a different matter.

He argued, "Anyone who isn't strong-willed enough to solve their own problems is a weakling." Being old-fashioned, European-bent and chauvinistic, he added, "I don't want my wife going around telling my private affairs to a stranger. If you need help, why haven't you gotten it from me?"

Fat chance. He didn't know beans about what was bothering me.

In spite of his protests, I went to Waco the following Tuesday. I had a bit of an argument getting permission to take the car the 20 miles, but Billie helped as much as she could by giving me moral support and caring for Todd.

As you can imagine, I was nervous. I didn't know what might evolve from this appointment; they might even put me in a hospital for the mentally insane. I had a lot of trepidations, but when I was shown into the office of the psychologist, Dr. Kenneth Bean, I began to feel completely at ease.

Dr. Bean was not a handsome man. In fact, he wore thick-lensed glasses which gave him the appearance of an owl. He was dark-headed and small of stature, and I don't think he walked as well as he should have. Upon reflection, he probably had spastic trouble. Nevertheless, I liked him.

We talked about my problems for a short time and then embarked on my difficulties with Ward. "But that's another matter," he said, "which we can get to later."

First, however, he wanted to give me some tests when I went in for my next appointment, which was to be a week later. "They'll be the Rorschach inkblots," he explained, "and I'll determine your inner turmoil by the way you interpret the pictures."

This sounded like fun. I was highly flattered that someone would give me this much time and concern for what I had always believed to be my own fault.

It was a relief, also, to know that I wasn't crazy, that I was just another person who had difficulties and probably nothing more than a minor mental illness. Dr. Bean gave me hope for the future, a future in which those thought demons wouldn't bother me for the rest of my life.

This was PSYCHOLOGY, about which I knew a little but had never had the opportunity to explore. It was like a miracle to me to realize that help was actually available.

When I left the little doctor's office that day, it must have been one of the happiest of my life. Since it was such a beautiful spring day, I decided to take a short walk around the campus to save the feelings of gladness and hope that I had in my heart. I didn't want those moments to end.

The mascots for the university were two cute bears. When I stopped by their enclosure, I realized that perhaps an end was in sight for the darkness and the heavy weight on my shoulders, that maybe I could be cured. Perhaps I wouldn't always do the wrong things anymore, and, just maybe, people would like me.

As I looked at those bears, I realized that I had found my doctor...

I had found psychotherapy and, through it...

I had found God, and

I had found hope and life.

CHAPTER 71

AFTER GAZING at the bear cubs and extending the relief as long as possible, I drove home with elation. I couldn't wait to tell Billie of my news. Ward was a different matter. When I tried to tell him how elated I was, he was scornful and told me I was "crazy" (which I already thought I was) and said I was foolish to believe that "quack."

Then, when I timorously told him that the doctor wanted to see him, he exploded saying, "Absolutely not! I'll never see him, and I'm not sure I'll let you go back!"

That really got to me, and I said, "I don't think you can stop me. I'm determined to see this out."

With that, he walked off to take a shower. But naturally I told Billie his reaction. She said to me, "You have to go. Leave it to me. I'll see that you go."

In an instant, my mood changed from forlorn to jovial. Perhaps it helped that we had moved to a smaller apartment down the hall, which was much more convenient and pleasant.

Todd grew to be fat and sassy and was a happy baby. He relished his bottle, and his favorite plaything was a man's hat. It covered his head down to his nose, but I guess he felt safe in that hat and it protected him from any stress his parents might be going through. The hat was his favorite plaything until he was two years old. When he was upset, he put the hat on his head. The nature of what he was doing was not lost on me, but having been reared in a house of turmoil, I didn't know what to do about it.

Ward and I continued to quarrel, and I ran him down about our not having any friends and being dissatisfied to the point he hit me. I don't blame him; I can be pretty vicious when I'm angry. I've learned to quell my temper. Added to the fact that we had no friends, Dr. Bean had dismissed me also because, as he said, "I build you up, and you go home to a husband who undoes all I accomplish."

Then to add to my discontent, Billie and her family had moved to a nearby city, so I didn't have anyone to talk to again. I did make friends with a woman named Katherine, who lived two blocks away, but she wasn't Billie.

Soon enough, we would move back to live close to my parents, but it wasn't enough to save our marriage.

CHAPTER 72

After I divorced Ward, life wasn't as easy as I thought it would be. I was fair game to everyone, especially the married men. One of my former junior college classmates called me and wanted a date. I angrily told him off in no uncertain terms. He then spread it around town: "Don't call her. She'll bite your head off." So, I didn't emerge as the desirable young girl I thought I would be after my divorce. And Ward took things pretty hard. He even promised me he'd go to the doctor with me if I would reconcile. Many times, I thought I should have given him that chance.

When we moved back home, I went back to work at the newspaper. I could always count on Richard to forgive and have no regrets. He needed me during the Christmas holidays and then I did such a good job, he kept me on. As my mental state worsened, added to my discontent with Ward, I began seeing a psychiatrist named Dr. Sartin in the nearby city. I liked him, and I would advise anyone who thinks they have a mental illness, or if there's someone in the family who acts strangely or worries a lot, to seek out a good doctor.

Dr. Sartin was recommended to me by my primary care physician and was highly thought of. He saw right away that Ward could be a problem for someone like me who was, frankly, a people-person and wanted to be noticed. I had had very little of that in my upbringing, and I didn't depend on myself at all. My parents thought that was their job. They'd even picked out and bought my china upon my marriage to Ward. It was not at all what I wanted but, now, I'm very fond of it.

Unfortunately, the good doctor came down with cancer and died, leaving me with no one yet again. I realized I needed more help and looked in the Yellow Pages for a new psychiatrist. By that time psychology was in vogue, and any doctor who had read a book or attended a seminar in psychology could call himself a "psychiatrist." There should have been more state licensing laws that determined whether or not these doctors qualified. As long as they practiced medicine, they could call themselves "psychiatrists." Even now, there's laxness in psychology requirements. As long as a person has a master's degree in psychology, they can practice psychotherapy—and at a great price to their patients both financially and mentally. Some of these psychologists earn even more than the psychiatrists, whose main function is to determine medications.

Dr. Reynaldo listed himself as a psychiatrist. He had no doubt read or heard of mind-effective drugs and gave me shots to unclutter my psyche. I wondered if my upbringing had to do with my confusion about myself—since I hadn't been diagnosed with OCD at that time—and asked the doctor what would make the difference in seeing the disease improve: drugs or environment. He answered that no matter what my parents did, I would have turned out the same. I found this hard to believe, especially after he told me that no matter what I did with Todd, without the drugs he would have problems. This confused me, and I had another "crisis." At the time, I taught a Sunday School class of fourth graders, and I was confused that anything I taught them would make an impression on their little personalities, so I had to give it up. I was also very confused about my effect on Todd, so I had what I called a "breakdown." Then I finally saw my primary doctor, and he told me not to go back to that "doctor," gave me a red medication to drink in milk and advised me to see him in a week.

I slept well that night for the first time in a month.

But I was obsessed with what Dr. Reynaldo had said about the new drugs and compulsively worried about them. This led to another crisis for me until I went to my own common-sense doctor whom I trusted. He admonished me for prescribing my own doctor and said I should have asked him before seeing someone else.

A week later I went back to see my primary-care doctor, and he said, "Why don't you consider moving away from here, especially from your parents who are driving you crazy, and are trying to run your life for you?" I knew what he said was true, especially in light of recent events.

A manager from the Lowe Theater Chain had recently opened a new drive-in movie theatre and sent a guy named Ed to manage it. Naturally, he came to the newspaper, where I was still working, for publicity and advertising, so I got acquainted with him. I liked him a lot in spite of his crippled leg due to Polio, so when he asked my little boy, who was three and a half years at the time and me, to go to the movies with him. I was happy to accept his offer, and, as soon as we were seated in his car, Todd said, "I smell chicken do-do." Well, we lived across the street from a hatchery, but I was embarrassed although Todd's remark certainly broke the ice.

Ed, Todd and I became a close threesome, and my parents asked Ed to come to dinner. They liked him a lot, mostly because he was so considerate of Todd. I liked Ed, too, but was hesitant about liking him too much because he was a cripple. I was also put off by my parents who invited Ed to join us every time they invited me to dinner. Then I began to think they liked him more because of Todd than me. However, in December, I came down with the flu, and Ed was quite attentive. When he asked me to marry him, I said "yes."

Later, I realized I was trying to please my parents more than I was trying to please myself. So, I broke my engagement. But my parents didn't give up. They would invite Ed to dinner at the same time they would invite Todd and me. On about the fourth such occasion that this happened, I arrived early and asked if Ed was coming. When they said "yes," I tearfully told them "You might gain a son, but you've lost a daughter." With that, I went home and didn't see them for a couple of weeks.

CHAPTER 73

WHAT THE DOCTOR talked about in relation to my parents' controlling me, made sense. Thus, I made plans to move to the city—about 150 miles away. One of my casual friends, Gladys, had already invited me to stay at her and her husband's home while I got settled but, before that, I made plans of my own. The first day I moved to the city, I found an efficiency apartment. Still, I hadn't counted on how much I would miss Todd. I had left him with my parents and gotten a job at Stanolind Oil Co, a branch of Standard Oil Co.

The first day on the job, one of the secretaries said I should meet her husband's brother, Casey. She added that we had a lot in common; he was recently divorced, had a little girl Todd's age, and lived in a small town of about 5,000 only 20 miles south. The small-town part appealed to me. I wanted to raise Todd in a town like the one I had grown up in. It was much safer and more fun. At least, I had enjoyed the good times when they occurred. Also, Casey was building a new general merchandise store which opened into his brother's appliance store. There was one catch. His mother, Lucy, was known to be the town battle-ax. She was hard to get along with, and I soon learned, had little good to say about anyone. By comparison, her dead doctor husband's sister, Hattie, who lived in her massive house, was sweet and never said a cross word about anyone. Hattie also cooked and kept the house clean, so Lucy managed to maintain a friendship.

In any regard, I married Casey, but it didn't last.

CHAPTER 74

MORE OPPORTUNITIES to date were on my horizon, but I was determined not to go out with anyone until my divorce from Casey was finalized. This commitment was a carry-over from my previous experience in not becoming involved while I was still married. I thought that was a sin. I remembered my experience with Richard, who was married and the worry over him was still fresh in my mind. After the divorce, I had several dates and the most outstanding one was with a Jewish guy I met at a nearby resort I had gone to with a couple of friends. His name was Herb, and I guessed I liked him because he was different. I had never met a Jewish man, so I was smitten. Anyhow, he knew I liked him and also that I was tolerant of his behavior, so he didn't treat me very nicely.

After my visits to the doctors and the treatment for my "thought trouble," my mental state had remained stable for a stretch. I had no major worries until I saw *The Bad Seed* which depicted an evil little girl and I began to worry about Todd again. I was consumed by the worry of medication vs. environment which was most important in rearing a child. My depression eventually led to my return to the newspaper back home.

Richard had a good heart when it came to one of his valued employees. He made a place for me, and even through our difficult times, I remember him for that. This time, I was to be the assistant to the news editor and, on the side, do his letters from time to time. He loved to write letters. I think it bolstered his ego and, for that, I resented it. I wanted to be a reporter, not a secretary. Unfortunately, that was the catalyst in us parting ways six years later.

My return home meant that I could be with Todd, even though I had my parents to contend with. They realized they had been too bossy and had interfered too much in my affairs, so they tried not to say anything about my activities. It was difficult having to take less money than I was earning in the city, and my circle of friends wasn't what I would consider upper-class. That was, not until Todd's second-grade teacher, Betty, realized I needed a group of high-class friends, the teachers' group, and invited me in.

Of course, with my ill-gotten friends before that, my parents couldn't hold back their displeasure. But, remembering what had happened before, I ignored them and went to night spots anyway. I did have the help of a psychiatrist, Dr. McElroy, who had been recommended by my physician. I knew I'd need help adjusting to the new situation so, this time, before I found myself lost and depressed, I asked for a referral. Dr. McElroy mostly listened to me and didn't prescribe medication, and I found simply talking to him helped.

Billie and her family had returned to town, and she had a new baby, Jennings III, who was 10 months old when I moved back in April. Billie was my bright spot and, thank goodness, we hadn't lost our sense of humor. After I got over the shock of moving back, life was pretty good. I had a job; I had Todd, and I had friends (the first group which my parents didn't approve of), and I had found a reputable psychiatrist. I don't think Dr. McElroy helped me a great deal, but he was there during the rough spots.

One such incident that he worked through with me occurred when I met a young man, who was quite good-looking, in one of my nightclub forays. By this time, I was sexually active on occasion, depending upon whether I liked the guy or not, but I was always careful that I was able to use my diaphragm or that the male had a condom. I didn't like this young man enough to have sex with him, so after dinner in a nearby town, when he suggested that he expected sex, I told him that I really wasn't interested. He said, "I didn't mean you had a choice and I want it RIGHT NOW!" I responded that I wasn't at all interested, that we were in the car, and that he didn't even have a condom. He said, "We'll do it anyway."

I knew he was serious, so I said, "Stop the car and let me out!" He stopped, but he still had sex on his mind. So, I quickly opened my door and got out but landed in a ditch full of water. I assessed the situation and knew I couldn't stay there, so I returned to the car and told him, "I'll do it if you'll get a condom." That seemed amenable to him, so we drove home, making a stop for the "necessities," and I had sex with him. But my mind wasn't on what I was doing; I only thought of the deed as survival. To my amazement, when he got ready to leave, he said, "Can I call you again?" As I was anxious to get rid of him, I said "yes." But when he called again, I said I was busy, and that ended the relationship.

I learned one thing from the experience: I didn't have

to like the person, and I could still use my body to get anything I wanted. As I've gotten older, I've changed my mind,
but it didn't help my reputation that I was so easy.

CHAPTER 75

I HUNG AROUND the teachers for two or three years, making lasting friendships. There were no lovers; all the males were either music or art teachers and gay. But I was particularly interested in one of them, a man named Brady, who was the music instructor at the high school. He was dashing, and I think he wanted to be interested in me but just didn't know how. He hated the way he was. I helped him with publicity for his music programs at the high school, and we got into the habit of him coming for Sunday dinner and dropping by every night after teaching private music classes.

Brady liked Todd and vice versa. I was sure Todd was safe from ribbing or a bad influence from any of the teacher-guys, but there was no father figure among them. Brady took us to dinner and bowling to pay back for all the Sunday dinners he had eaten at our house.

Then Rick entered the picture. He was new in town; having come to manage the garment factory his father was getting too old to manage. Rick was a devout Catholic, rich, a graduate of Georgetown University Law School, and mean. I was immediately taken with him, but he told me on our third date that he couldn't marry me because of my two previous divorces. Also, his parents, who had come from Ireland, didn't approve of me. And he would do anything his parents wanted him to do. Why else was he running the garment factory when he would rather be practicing law? I guess the circumstance of having to be on the job every day at the factory was frustrating to him, but I think he was just a spoiled brat with a mean streak.

He was the same age as I was but not a father-figure at all to Todd. He didn't even like him and called him "Turdy-Todd." Todd, of course, didn't like him either and urged me not to go out with him. My father took it upon himself to call and warn me of the evils of the Catholic-Irish, especially Rick, but I wouldn't listen. I wish I had. For once, he was right.

Rick knew that I liked him and would overlook anything he did, even to the point of making my life miserable. But there was no one in town to take his place, even though I did break up with him several times. I began to drink a lot to keep up with him—unbridled Scotch and water. My friends noticed I was drinking too much, especially the teachers, and talked to me about what it was doing to Todd. I listened to them and in an effort to get away from Rick, went with two of my girlfriends to a nearby resort town for the weekend.

I found I could have fun without Rick and without drinking so much, and I met a nice guy, Virgil. He lived in a neighboring state, was in the construction business as a welder and he wanted to see me again. He came the next week and then we had a date to meet halfway at one of my friend's house. He was quite late, which should have been a warning to me, but in comparison to the way Rick treated me, it was a small infraction. Ultimately, I dismissed it as what you put up with when dating.

Virgil came to see me quite often after that and was usually on time. Rick didn't like it and was more attentive to me as a result. During all this, Dr. McElroy moved to Texas, and I was turned over to Dr. Brown, who was the leading psychiatrist in the area. He only charged $10 an hour—expensive medicine in those days. I couldn't afford the $10, so we agreed that I would pay $5 upfront and the remainder after I was finished. (He didn't know that at age 90 I would still be seeing psychiatrists.)

Soon enough, I saw cracks in Virgil's personality. I went with him to his home one day and immediately liked his mother and son, Chuck, who lived with his own mother, Virgil's ex-wife, but I didn't take to his religion which was based on racism. Virgil hated African-Americans and Jews and didn't like the fact I was seeing Dr. Brown, who was a "dirty Jew," according to Virgil. Still, I overlooked his opinion as something minor.

Actually, I was becoming fonder of Virgil and seeing him more often. Rick didn't like this at all and became even more attentive. One weekend he even took me to a resort town, and we had a nice time, but my mind was on Virgil. The following week, Rick said, "Why don't we get married secretly and not tell my parents, then when they find out, they'll have to accept you?"

Without hesitation, I told him, "No way! If I can't be married openly, I'm not interested!"

Two days later it would be the Fourth of July, and I intended to spend it with Virgil. On the night of July 3, I was with Rick, but when he took me home, Virgil had just driven up. Rick said, "I'm not going to let you go with him. This is my date!" And with that, he drove on by, with Virgil in hot pursuit. Rick led him all over town, but I knew the decision was up to me. So, I implored Rick to take me home. I knew during the drive that Virgil was best for me as Rick had never caused me anything but heartache. He reluctantly drove me home, and I finally bid him good-bye...for a while anyway.

CHAPTER 76

VIRGIL WON the race and the heart of the fair maiden.

The next morning at breakfast, he said, "Why don't we just get married?" I accepted marriage proposals like I would dance invitations, so I said "OK." Had I thought about it, I would have surmised it wasn't a good idea at all, but there were two motives involved:

For Virgil, it meant he wouldn't have to worry about my involvement with Rick.

For me, it would get me out of my mess with Rick.

All I had to do was get a dress on and pack an overnight bag. Since the Fourth was on Thursday, I didn't plan to work the following two days either. Todd would be safe with my parents. I didn't think ahead. In fact, I had several drinks of Scotch and soda to bolster my decision. Off we went to his hometown with a couple who were quite close to him to serve as witnesses, and we were married by a justice of the peace. The justice of the peace wasn't happy about marrying us—I guess because we were under the influence.

I don't want to tell you the furor we incurred back home, but first, we had to explain to Rick, then my family, the office, and all my friends what had transpired. Surprise marriages are not well thought of. The happiest individual was Todd, who liked Virgil and was afraid I would inflict Rick on him.

Then the future loomed in front of us. Virgil was going to take a job in the state of Nevada, so I would either have to go with him or stay in my rented house and keep my job. Then I figured out Todd couldn't be changing schools every time Virgil took a job and moved to a new state. Virgil suggested I leave Todd with my parents, but I knew what that entailed. I said "No" immediately. That was the end of the discussion. We fixed another Scotch and soda and watched television instead.

The first of the following week, Virgil went back to his job in the city, and I set about working. I carried on as usual with my teacher friends and left Rick to lick his wounds. Friday, I had several of the teachers over when Virgil came home, and he didn't like that at all. He made his dislike of the situation known, so my friends left. I was angry and told him I was lonesome and didn't want to give up my friends, but he said, "You've got Todd." I argued that I'd had Todd before we were married, and he wasn't enough. So, as was our way, we made another Scotch and soda and forgot about it.

The next week Virgil came home on Saturday, but quite late and spent what seemed to me a long time in the shower. He continued coming home Saturday evenings but decided to play golf on Sundays. At first, he played nine holes; then he went around a second time, and finally, he graduated to three rounds of golf. My complaints didn't do any good, and the catalyst came when he didn't come home until Sunday and then went to the golf course.

This was not acceptable behavior, not even to one as tolerant as I was. Add to that stress his "religion," which was a hate-group in disguise and the relationship was untenable. Also, he held disdain for my Jewish doctor, who I knew I needed. After the Sunday where he enjoyed his third round of golf, I decided I was better off without him, and no liquor of any kind was going to solve my problems. He promised to come home late Saturday, so I waited up to tell him our marriage wasn't working. But it wasn't just his extended games of golf that had me thrown; I didn't trust him because the week before when I'd tried to call him Saturday at his motel, the girl who was working there said, "Virgil isn't up yet." I told her, "Well, this is MRS. Virgil and you can go wake him up!" *She was a little too familiar.*

The next morning when I was leaving for work, we told each other goodbye with tears in our eyes. I did care for him and felt he cared for me. We plainly had too many problems. From the Fourth of July to Halloween was all the marriage lasted. I vowed to know the next one—if there was one—better and have a few plans laid out. I felt like a failure—again(!) for quite some time.

CHAPTER 77

BILLIE TOLD MY PARENTS about Virgil's leaving, and I think they were relieved.

Virgil had bought me a new washer and dryer when we were first married. We JUST had to have one, he intoned. But guess who was left to make the payments? Although, he did pay for the divorce.

I felt pretty low after he left, but not for long. The teachers surrounded me with their caring ways, and we had a new mathematics teacher in our midst—Dustin. He taught in the school system at Parsons City, a little town about five miles away. I had written about him when he was at Vermillion High School, about seven miles from Mooresville in the other direction. He was good-looking, smart, the valedictorian of his class, and musically inclined. And he was not gay! I noticed his attention toward me even when we had outings, but I had been married to Virgil then.

On the Monday before Thanksgiving, he had a dinner party in his apartment at Parsons City with Marvin Crain, Beverly Black and me as guests. Beverly liked Marvin, even though he was a little on the feminine side (they later married and had two lovely daughters), so they paired off. That left just Dustin and me, and his attention was obvious. When I was ready to go home, he asked if he could follow me "So you'll be safe," he said. I agreed. Sure, I liked Dustin, but I was 10 years older than his 24. And He was nearly eleven years older than Todd, which left him stuck in the middle.

Dustin followed me home, and we kissed goodnight after he had told me he was sorry about my experience with Virgil, that I looked so sad, and would I consider going out with him Saturday night? I quickly said "yes," although I reminded him that I was 10 years older. He said that didn't matter and he would call me before the weekend. Dustin was cute, funny, and intelligent. He made me forget Virgil, and he was good in bed.

But things weren't so good at the office. Richard kept wanting me to do more and more letters for him, even though I had appointments elsewhere for news stories.

We had moved to a new building Richard had built, but it was cold. There was friction between us about the temperature, not to mention the letters. Billie and I suggested a girl who was very efficient as a secretary, but, after giving her a try, Richard gleefully told us she wouldn't do. He was almost happy that she didn't work out, so I would have to do them. Things were pretty sticky around there, and you could cut the tension with a knife. Then one Monday morning, a new girl showed up, presumably to take my job. Billie, who was society editor, assessed the situation, then walked off and went home. I wished I could have followed suit, but I didn't have a husband to support me, so I had to stay.

Richard was known for never firing anyone, but he could make life so miserable they'd quit, this in turn because he didn't want to pay unemployment insurance. This was enough of an impetus for me to look for another job, but Richard was so powerful in that small town, the word was "don't hire Richard's girls, or you'll make an enemy of him." No one wanted to get on his bad side. That meant I had to put up with his torture. Looking back, I can say the reason I was always cold was the result of the situation, and I have never liked to be cold since. This was a symptom of the OCD, and it haunted me in every job I had. It was a matter of control. Since I wouldn't do his letters, the end result was control of the temperature. I took to wearing a coat and, since my feet were cold, I brought a little throw rug to put under them. I couldn't think clearly, and I don't know how I got through the days.

Since all these new events in my life had transpired, Dr. Brown had suffered a nervous breakdown. He couldn't practice. I kept asking when he was coming back to work, and his secretaries assured me it would be soon, but when I needed him, he wasn't there.

One bright spot was Dustin. He was caring and understanding, and he surprised me one day in January, right after my divorce, by proposing. He had received a scholarship to Purdue University and wanted to take Todd and me with him. I reminded him of the age difference, and that I had made mistakes in judgment before and didn't want to louse up again.

CHAPTER 78

DUSTIN KNEW ONE THING: He didn't want to lose me. I made the mistake of saying I might apply for a news editor job at *The Weekly* at Parsons City. He thought that was a good idea, but, I was hesitant. Frankly, I wanted to get as far away from Richard as possible but, I was certain I didn't want to go to Lafayette with Dustin while he pursued his education. In those days, you had to be married, and I didn't want that either.

I took a different avenue when I noticed an ad for a news editor at two weeklies published by The Tri-Lakes Press in Branson, Mo. I called them immediately, made an appointment, went for an interview, and got the job. I was to start in two weeks since I explained I wanted to give two-weeks' notice and had some appointments to keep. I moved to Branson and, the first week, did a bang-up job with both papers, much to my new boss's pleasure. This was the early part of April, and I had decided to let Todd stay with my folks to finish the school year. Then I wanted him with me.

Rick had re-entered the picture in January after hearing all about the trouble at the newspaper, and he asked me to go to lunch. Dustin didn't like that one bit and was jealous. He didn't want me to see him at all and couldn't be consoled when I did. I promised I wouldn't see Rick, but Dustin was angry, anyway, because I hadn't applied at the Parsons City newspaper, and had moved away from Mooresville. His bosses in the Parsons City School District didn't want to lose him, so they pointed out the age difference and the fact that I had been married three times and was a poor risk. Their words must've sunk in because Dustin broke up with me, much to my unhappiness. He didn't take advantage of the offer at Purdue but instead took a job in California. I was distraught and wished I could have married him, but his proposal came too soon after Virgil.

I busied myself with my work and got over him. Rick came to see me at least once every two weeks, but it wasn't the same. I was wiser, and he couldn't hurt me. Also, he had met a new Catholic girlfriend, who had never been married, and his parents approved of her. I didn't even care. And I liked my new job. Branson was good for me. I was successful, which I hadn't experienced much in my life. I was there before the theaters were built in Branson by the stars who moved there—and loved every minute of it. It was a pretty country with a few tourist attractions, catering to those who just wanted to get away and enjoy themselves. I would say Branson was a "party town" at the time. At least, I had a good time, and I would rather have lived there than anyplace on the Earth. But it's too late now.

Branson had everything, except eligible men. I found the one most non-eligible at a night spot with friends when Fred came in. He had on a nice shirt, quality trousers, and wingtip shoes, which were fashionable for the times. He had lots of sandy hair and was tall and cute. I went up to the bar to chat with him, told him who I was and what I did, and asked him to call me. After I sat down, an older woman, and a Branson character who knew what went on around the town walked by my table and said to me, "Cool-It, Clyde." So, I was forewarned about Fred (Cool-It, Clyde), although I didn't know the details.

I learned later that Fred and alcohol didn't mix, he was insanely jealous and hard to get rid of. He couldn't take rejection. One of the better restaurants in town had already barred him from coming in, although the owner told me I could come anytime, but "just don't bring Fred." He was also a mama's-boy, and while he didn't work when I met him, I soon learned where he got his spending money— from his mother. But Todd liked him, and he liked Todd.

We made a nice foursome—Fred, Todd, Tuck (our new dog) and me, and life ran smoothly for about a year. Fred finally got a job with a land developer, and one night there was a cookout at his boss's home. Fred had too much to drink, and I found out what "Cool-It, Clyde" meant. He thought I was paying too much attention to his boss and backhanded me on the way home. After we got to my house, he choked me. I was able to scream, so he stopped in case I might have been heard. I immediately scurried out of his grasp and threatened to call the police if he didn't leave, so he left.

But, as I had heard, he *was* difficult to get rid of. He lurked around my house several times, and each time I called the police, so he left. But once he took Tuck with him. Todd was very upset, and I reported it to the police. The next day, I saw Fred's car parked downtown with Tuck in the back seat. Tuck went willingly with me to the office. I don't know what Fred thought when he came back to the car, and I refused to talk to him on the phone. He was afraid to come around me since I called the police frequently. Mercifully, he stayed away.

But one night I wasn't so lucky as to escape his clutches. I was with friends at a nightclub when Fred came in, in an obvious bad mood brought on by alcohol. My friends said that it was best to leave before Fred lost his temper again upon seeing me. We were on our way out when Fred accosted me again. He forced me down on a table, said he had "lived with me and had sex with me," and began choking me. One of my friends forced him off and walloped him good. We left but Fred called me at my office the next morning, and I agreed to meet him at a nearby restaurant to talk. I told him I would never talk to him again, that he was to leave me alone or I would file charges against him. He seemed to know that I meant what I said. I saw him once after that, and we didn't speak to one another. Thank goodness, Fred was finally history.

After Fred, there were various boyfriends, none serious except one: Chuck Crosby. A native of Branson, he taught in a neighboring high school. Chuck was good-looking AND intelligent, something I had missed in the others. We began a relationship as lovers but ended as friends, mainly because he was separated from his wife and desperately wanted to reconcile with her. That left me as the weekend aversion. I soon learned we would be nothing more than friends. At that time, that was OK with me. I needed a friend to tell me what to do.

I discovered Dr. Brown was obviously not going to return to his practice. In short, he went completely bonkers. Instead, his office advised me I should see Dr. Francis Jones, his psychologist, in the same office. I liked Dr. Jones and kept in touch with him even after I left Branson. I guess he's dead now or retired since he was about my age. In the meantime, I had applied for a job as the news editor of a daily in a town of about 6,000 in Clay Center, Kansas. The publisher flew me there for an interview and hired me on the spot. Todd wanted me to take the job, even though he was popular in school. Chuck also urged me to take the job since all the available men in Branson were "sub-standard" and not my type.

Chuck also knew about Dr. Jones and thought it was a smart plan to see him. He said some of my doctors had helped me in the past.

Since I had been a little wild when I was in Branson, Dr. Jones recognized the wrong paths I was taking and urged me to take the job at Clay Center.

I did make the move and wound up 250 miles away from my home, my way of life, and my doctors. And then, unsurprisingly, I was homesick. Compared to Branson, Clay Center was a prison. Kansas was a dry state; the bars only sold 3.5 percent beer, there was no place to go, and there were no hot, single men. It was no wonder when Dr. Huffman showed me attention that I got involved. Kent, as I called him, was off-and-on separated from his wife, but he didn't want to get a divorce because it would cost him a lot of money. I reasoned I had left my doctors behind and he had taken their place. But he didn't see it the same way. I was fodder for his appetite and, I learned later, he had bedded most of his patients. Instead of the good life, I sought in the town for Todd and me, I became a pariah. I'm sorry for letting Todd down and missing my opportunity for a respectful place in the community if I would only have behaved.

I wanted out.

Mr. Thompson, my boss, was taken aback after I told him I was resigning my job and moving to Edwardsville, Illinois, after having worked for him only 10 months. I took a job as wire editor and assistant to the news editor, anything to get away from Clay Center and the doctor. But he followed me over in his twin-engine plane, visiting most weekends. I found I wasn't a good mistress because I wanted to be married.

Besides, I had met a man, Mike, on a trip to Branson just before I moved to Edwardsville. Mike had an appliance store in Stanton, Illinois, and asked if he could call. I thought he was a little old for me but found later he was the same age as the doctor. He called two weeks after I moved, and we went out on a Saturday night. I liked him very much and, as he was leaving, he said, "Dear, let's go to bed." Well, that was the nicest way anyone had ever asked. I protested a bit, but he eventually won me over—and on the first date, which was a first for me. I knew I'd see him again...

Yet, I was anxious in my new role and city. I didn't like Edwardsville. I wasn't the "big cheese" at the newspaper; the paper wasn't considered "good" by the townspeople; I wasn't in love with either Mike or Kent, and I didn't have an able psychiatrist. I was lost, and never put down roots. To boot, I had problems making friends, and I didn't go to church where I could have made them. Just before I moved on, I went to a church group meeting and, for the first time since I had been there, felt important and at home. I thought *that's what I should have done from the beginning.* But at the time, and despite coming late to the party, so to speak, I didn't have much quality of life. Again, I drank too much, thanks to Mike. He once said, "Alcohol plays a big part in my life." It sure did, and it played a huge role in all of his friends' lives who were the big businessmen.

In spite of my struggles, I did buy a house and enjoyed fixing it up. It was a two-story brick, four bedrooms upstairs, circa 1920. I read an article in the newspaper later that these houses could even be ordered from Sears, Roebuck, complete with instructions on how to put them together. I don't think my house was "put together" with glue and a few nails, but it was interesting to know.

Mike's friend, Al, was instrumental in getting me a good deal on central air conditioning, and the house, which had a basement, was centrally heated. So, I enjoyed that for a while but still was restless and dissatisfied. The doctor I was assigned to at the Mental Health Clinic in Granite City, Illinois, adopted Mike's viewpoint in our relationship, so I finally asked for another doctor who would pay attention to my problems. He didn't describe my condition as OCD; in fact, he didn't diagnose it at all. But he was kind. As I think back, I don't even remember his name, so I know he didn't make much of an impression on me.

The newspaper was run inefficiently, and I wasn't proud to work there. So, I started looking elsewhere and found a paper I liked in Wilmington, Del. This position was on the editorial desk, which I thought I knew something about. I came for an interview and was hired. The news people at Edwardsville were shocked when I told them I was leaving, especially since I had bought my house only a year and a half ago. I was leaving Mike and the doctor behind, but the therapist at the Mental Health Center finally came through and told me to go. He said, "You're obviously not going to marry Mike, and I think you'll like the big city. There'll be more opportunity for you there." After much thought and difficulty, I decided to lease the house, with the option to buy, to a woman who wanted to turn it into a day nursery. Then I packed and left.

I arrived in Wilmington on January 3, 1970, by myself and I cried most of the way there. Even though I wasn't sure I was doing the right thing, it turned out, I was.

One good thing happened while I was in Edwardsville. About the second Christmas I lived there, I received a note from Dr. Brown's office that read:

"We've noted you paid on your bill month after month diligently, so we're canceling the remainder of your account with your last payment. We hope you and your son have a Merry Christmas."

It pays to be honest.

Another note I received was from Todd's dad, who hadn't been involved with Todd much in his life. Ward told my dad that "it hurt too much to see Todd," and I don't think he realized what it did to Todd. He had decided he wanted to pay for Todd's college expenses if I would be responsible for his allowance.

This was a good turn of events.

I liked my job, and the newspaper was well thought of, so I was a sort of celebrity when I told others I worked there. People thought I must have been pretty smart to be a reporter. My job on the editorial desk wasn't much fun, but I persisted even though my bosses didn't think I was the best. The first time a reporter's job came up, I applied for it and was able to make the change. Now, in the Women's Department, I liked my boss, Bette McNear. In fact, we remained friends until she died about four years ago. The other women in the department were lovely, too.

CHAPTER 79

I MET PAUL at a Parents Without Partners discussion group, and we were married five weeks later. But our speedy courtship wasn't that simple. I was going to visit my parents over the Memorial Day holiday, and he wanted to go, too. I told him, "They live in the country in a small two-bedroom house, so you'd either have to sleep on the couch or in a motel." He thought that over a minute and said, "We'll just get married." That was my proposal. After we got married, we spent the next year getting acquainted.

Paul was my funny husband. Our marriage lasted 31 years and would have lasted longer had he not died of cancer. He made me laugh a lot, especially with his fart jokes. The first time he expelled wind (there's always a first time after the nuptials), he claimed he was killing "fart bugs." The second time, he said, "this place is infested with fart bugs." It always amazed me how he could fart and hit the floor at the same time.

He had five children, three from his first marriage, and two young boys; five and 10, from his second marriage to

Dr. Eva Weltin, a psychiatrist, for whom he ran errands. He was very genteel in front of his children, and they had no knowledge about the "fart bugs." In fact, they had very little knowledge about what made me laugh concerning his crude habits. We entertained a lot and Paul would say, "Don't forget to invite Lord and Lady Fartsalot." He knew how to amuse me.

But there were problems, some his fault, some mine. His main problem was named Eva, the doctor. She had hoped they'd get back together, but then I came along. Paul's sister, Evelyn, said Eva was "devastated" when she learned he had remarried. She set out to sabotage the marriage. Perhaps being a psychiatrist compelled her to take the odd actions she did, or maybe it was just inherent that she was a woman, but she persisted in calling Paul every night at about 10:15 to give instructions about what he was supposed to do the next day concerning the two young boys. She knew that would upset me.

Finally, four years later, I answered the phone one night and, of course, it was Eva. I said, "You have the wrong number" and didn't put the phone back on the cradle because I knew she would call again. I didn't want Paul to know what had occurred, though I expected him to find out sooner or later. In her Hungarian accent, she said, "I do not have the wrong number..." But I hung up anyway. I must admit, I was extremely jealous of her looks and being smart enough to have mastered the English language to become a psychiatrist.

Of course, she called Paul the next day at his office and told him what had happened. He said, "She has a right to protect her home. From now on, you'll just have to call me at the office."

I was in control, and it was little wonder that I had to see a psychiatrist early in our marriage. That was the nearest I came to cracking up, in my long history of mental illness. I truly couldn't handle the situation, although the psychiatrist I saw was another foreigner and very jealous of Eva also. Her name was Lydia Bales, and she was from Brazil. She didn't do me much good and was instead too interested in what Eva was doing. She was never on time and made me miss the first two hours of work every Monday morning. I finally stopped seeing her and got the name of another psychiatrist from my primary doctor.

Paul discovered early on that isolating himself bothered me a great deal. I treated his behavior as though he had abandoned me. When he was angry with me, he would punish me by not talking to me, or withdrawing himself completely. Todd noticed it and once asked me if a visit I had made to the psychiatrist helped. I didn't become angry very easily, but when we had a disagreement, I quickly wanted to make up rather than have to endure the pain of isolation. Anything was better than that, even though I had to undergo emotional abuse again. Most of my husbands knew this about me.

While Paul knew my psychiatric background before we were married, he went through a period where he hinted that he wished he hadn't married me with all my problems. But since he had been married to a psychiatrist, he knew quite a bit about psychiatry and was helpful at times. I would say, most of the time in our 31-year marriage he was sympathetic toward my seeing a doctor.

During our third year of marriage, Bette McNear was replaced by a guy who was not sympathetic to my needs at all. It began the second year I was in the Women's Department when one of the women, whose desk was on the window-side of the office, persisted in opening the window. My desk position, on the opposite side of the room, caught the cold air the most. I protested a great deal but to no avail. I hated cold air (it signified to me that I was losing control of the situation). So, I moved to an empty desk in the Sports Department, which adjoined our department, much to the consternation of everyone in the women's group as well as those in the Sports Department. I'm sure the news of my action spread all over the building.

It didn't take long for the new guy to quickly access the situation. He called me into a private office one Monday morning and asked for my resignation. I was shocked, and the severance pay of about $1500 didn't ease my pain. One editor later told me over a drink that the reason for my dismissal was that I was "difficult."

I took a job with Family Court as stenographer for the chief judge, who I did not like. Actually, I didn't like anybody in a position of authority over me, and I'm surprised I wasn't fired. But I was lucky. I received a scholarship to go back to college to finish my degree in criminal judgment and psychology, going to class twice a week and two weekends a month. Paul was very proud of me, but I think my parents resented the fact that I was learning more knowledge than they had. Of course, I had to make many trips to the doctor during that time. Then I became a mediator at the court, which was prestigious, too, but not as much as working for the *News-Journal*.

As time went on, I liked my job even more so than working for the newspaper. But Paul, who was nine years older, had retired from his job as a new car salesman and wanted me to retire after eight years of mediating when I reached 60 years of age. I did, and we traveled a lot until his death in 2001.

During the time I was married to Paul, I was treated by my favorite doctor, Dr. Steg, for about eight years. He's the one who finally diagnosed me with obsessive-compulsive disorder and tried hard to help me. He did not try to "cure" me, it should be noted, but wanted to help me. I don't think there is a cure for mental illness, but it can be controlled. A mental illness has so many facets to it; it's difficult to treat. I saw Dr. Steg three times a week, and he showed me how to get my illness under control.

I learned to think various thoughts that would put the worry to rest. One of the ways I used was that "I have thought this through once before, so I don't have to think of it again." I related this to a book I had read, where the mother incessantly told her son to "Shut up, Kester" and that made sense to me. I would tell myself, "Shut up, Kester" and that would serve to curtail the thought. Whenever I could see "thought trouble" coming, I learned to say "now" to apprehend the problem. These methods didn't work all the time, and when they didn't, I would have a worry on my mind all day long before it was resolved.

Those were bad days for me, and the treatment wasn't easy. Later, I realized these challenges coincided with my menopausal days and, while I never really had any indications of menopause, that must have been the reason why it was so difficult.

Dr. Steg retired and moved to Florida after my retirement, but I continued to go to him until he left. I heard from him on my birthday and sent a brief note on his. (I was eight days older than he.) He had a stroke and died a few years ago. His wife wrote to tell me about it.

SECTION
FOUR

LIFE AFTER
Diagnosis

CHAPTER 80

I HAVE LEARNED that patients with OCD learn early to hide their illness from others. I formerly had lunch on Fridays with a friend, Chris, for several years and once she told me, "I've watched you closely, and you don't act like you have a mental illness." I told her that I had learned to hide it.

After Dr. Steg, I went to Dr. Straughn who was interested in my case but who I considered to be a "society" doctor. He lived in a posh neighborhood behind the art museum and, while he took Medicare, he made me fill out the forms until Medicare balked and he had to fill them out himself. I liked him, but there was no lasting friendship like what had occurred with Dr. Steg after he retired. He taught art at the Lifelong Learning Center and wanted nothing to do with his former patients.

Dr. Steg recommended a doctor I didn't like and didn't think was doing me any good. This led me to a state of confusion until I saw an advertisement in the newspaper that stated the Wellness Center had moved its office to a new address in Concord Plaza. I thought I would give them a try since I was getting more and more psychotic with the other doctor. Fortunately, I went to a therapist there, who moonlighted as a psychologist on evenings from her day job as a school psychologist. I say "fortunately" because Paul died two weeks later, and they saw me through it. I also saw a psychiatrist once every two weeks, and I still see him. I was also changed over to a psychologist, Gail Tolpin, after a year and I continue to see her as well.

After Paul's death, I met Jim Watson by chance—through social media. My step-daughter, Marilyn, was visiting, and, while looking at her laptop to see who had contacted her on Match.Com, suggested we find someone for me within a 50-mile radius. This was in July the December after Paul had died. I wasn't so sure I wanted to meet anyone, but said, "I'll give it a try."

Jim lived in Chalfont, PA. He was not handsome but still good-looking. Having been educated at Purdue University, he was retired from American Express as a financial adviser. I wrote a short note, not telling him I was a former newspaperwoman (he might have thought I was writing an expose on media dating) but told him I was from Missouri. I ended by telling him "I have all my teeth and they're good."

Apparently, he liked my sense of humor as he wrote back the next day, saying he was letting his ear-hair grow so he could have a comb-over. We wrote to each other for about two months before meeting for dinner. Dating experts say you should meet at a public place, but I wasn't afraid of him. He came to the house. I didn't think the father of two young boys, 13 and 17, would do anything untoward. I was more concerned about whether or not he had a ponytail and wore white socks. Thankfully, he turned out to be a regular guy, and I liked him.

Jim was all I wanted barring one catch: He was witty, cool, confident and nice-looking, but he lived in Pennsylvania. His sons didn't want to move to Delaware, and I didn't want to move to Pennsylvania. I almost did, but then broke the engagement rather than opting to relocate. We waited four years to get married when both boys were enrolled at Penn State. It was a bumpy four years, but I had Dr. Obeidy, and Gail, to see me through it. I changed my mind many times until Jim said he was a decent, religious man with high standards and he was tired of my insecurities and doubts. Then we set the date for May 13, when school was almost out and found an eight-room house with breezeway, attached garage, and full basement. I was in love with the house; also, in love with Jim.

The two boys were distant with me but warmed up as the years went by. Both of them now have good jobs and Alex, the younger one, is married and has a baby girl born in March 2018. He has a lovely wife, Sarah, who has a doctorate in ENT. Jim also has two older boys, Eric, who is a tennis pro in Phoenix, and Robert, who married an Australian girl and lives in her native country.

The marriage to Jim was happy, but he liked to be in control. The three years we were married were plagued with his illnesses, and he finally had a knee replacement in January of 2009. But in May, he was diagnosed with leukemia and died on July 11, 2009. Both Eric and Robert were present, and I was heartbroken. I cried every night for a long time thinking about him. Jim was fine with my doctors and encouraged me to go see them. He did tell me one time, after an argument, that I could be mean. I guess I *could* be a dirty fighter, but I was quick to get over it. I was always sorry for the things I said.

CHAPTER 81

I MET RAGHBIR the following July on Match.Com. My friend, Kathie, with whom I made greeting cards, saw me through my grief with Jim and was actively dating several guys she'd met online. She's younger than I, prettier, and has a bubbly personality, so she had no trouble meeting men. She's dated a lot of "frogs," but a few "princes" also came along. Raghbir didn't show me much in his photo and resume, so I skipped over him. But he wrote to me, then called, and later I thought he was angling for a "fixed-marriage" orchestrated by his son, who was also named Paul. Paul thought his dad needed more activity after his wife, an American girl, had died four years previously.

Raghbir was a native of India but came to this country as a young man to go to Purdue University, (I should have stock in Purdue; that's No. 3) from which he had a doctor's degree in engineering. He also had a lot of money, if you could call $1M a lot. (I could.) He was very sweet to me, was dependable in calling and seeing me, and liked to travel. So, did I, so we took a trip to Cancun in October 2010. He made me laugh a lot, so I decided I would marry him. He had already decided he wanted to marry me and had three diamond engagement rings made into a single band. He proposed after we got back from Cancun. I said "yes," and we set the date for May 13, 2011, when my stepson and his partner, Randy and Jeff, would be in Delaware.

I went to see my friend, Mary Belle Hall Cross, during the Christmas holidays in Palm Desert, CA., and Raghbir called every day at one o'clock on the dot. He also called me "my love," which was hard to resist. Raghbir was about my height with brown eyes and a neatly trimmed gray beard and gray hair. I was proud to take him to church and, because of Raghbir and his attention, was called a "hot lady" by one of Mary Belle's friends, Sally, who added, "I'll be glad when you're gone. You're too much competition."

We were married in May, and I was very happy. I thanked God for my luck in finding such a sweet man, not to mention the newfound security I had been blessed with. But Raghbir was restless, and I could see why. He and his late wife wrote a number of novels and had them published. He needed to be creative. I told him we should go to his house in Catonsville, MD, outside Baltimore, and get his computer and notes so he could write again. But his son, who was living in the house, said we couldn't come for six weeks because he "wasn't ready." I don't know what he planned to do; the house belonged to Raghbir. Trouble was coming in the form of Paul.

When his dad suffered a slight stroke in June, about a month after we were married, I called Paul to tell him, and he told me to take him to the emergency room at the hospital. He wasn't there very long, and the results of the stroke weren't apparent. We planned to take a trip across Canada by rail but, in the meantime, Raghbir was getting his will ready and wanted to leave me the interest from a trust. The law firm attorney we engaged said they didn't do trusts and we would have to go to a firm that specialized in them. I told Paul on the phone about our plans, and I noticed he was standoffish about the idea. This was just one trust; he would, of course, get the rest. I really didn't think it would be much; just enough to make up the difference if we went to a retirement home to live, which we had already discussed.

Well, I guess Paul saw dollar signs slipping away from him and going to me, but what did he expect? Did he have the idea that I would take care of his dad and leave him with no responsibility? I guess so. The daughter, Sandra, who lived in Phoenix, had already had a falling out with Paul and her father and was out of the will. That meant Paul would get it all—until I came along. It was obvious what his mindset was when Paul called the next day, and I answered and said, "How are you?" He answered curtly, "Very well, thank you. Could I please speak to my dad?"

I don't know what went on between them, but he surprised us (or so I thought) and came Monday for a visit. Instead, he said, "I came to take my Dad home!"

I was stunned.

Then Raghbir told me, "I called him last night and I'm going with him."

I asked, "You're leaving me?" And Paul reiterated, "I'm taking my dad home." He said that several times as if to make sure I'd heard him.

I heard him the first time.

I was beyond astonished. We had been so happy, or so I thought. Only Raghbir wasn't as happy as I thought.

Then Raghbir said, "I forgot. I have a doctor's appointment Friday." Paul answered him, "There are plenty of doctors in Maryland."

They left.

I crumpled, unable to believe what had happened.

But apparently, it had.

Kathie came over to console me, but it was a long time before I could face the truth.

I only heard from Raghbir three times by phone. The second time he called, which was the following Sunday, he asked for a friend's number, and I said, "What do you want that for?"

He said, "So I can call to see how you are."

I said, "Why don't you just call me? I'll tell you."

He answered, "Paul won't let me. He's afraid you'll talk me into coming back."

I have to say this about Raghbir: He was honest.

That was September 12, 2011. We had only been married four months.

The next time I heard from Raghbir was late in November. At that time, he told me to go ahead and get a divorce. I did, and that was the end.

Which brings me to the present.

CHAPTER 82

ONCE, before he died, I was sitting in the living room with Paul, my husband, basking in the glory of our relationship.

I said, "Aren't you glad I went to all those doctors after I left the newspaper? Now, I'm OK, instead of being so difficult."

He said flatly, "You're still difficult."

All of my husbands, with the exception of Ward, approved of my going to see psychiatrists/psychologists; I guess they hoped I would improve and saw no harm in going. Ward did say when he wanted to reconcile, that he would see my doctor and I often wish I had given him the chance. On the other hand, I sometimes have wondered what I would have accomplished had I stayed with him and not have had the opportunities I did to see good doctors and take their recommended medications.

As learned as Dr. Steg was, and especially considering the fact he had a medical degree, I'm somewhat disappointed that he didn't prescribe medication. It wasn't until I began seeing Dr. Obeidy in 2001 that I was given Effexor and Clonazepam, which are anti-depressants and work wonders with OCD. Now, when I have a disturbing thought, I know the medications will not let it become a big problem and that I will soon forget it. Formerly, the thought would catch hold, and I would have to resolve it. Otherwise, I couldn't go on with my everyday life. It was like a clam or leach that would attach itself to my brain.

But I did feel hopeful after I first saw Dr. Bean, although he presented a threat to Ward. Ward was from the old school where women weren't too important except to have children and to keep the house going. Ward once told me (toward the end of our marriage), "I work for the money and it's mine. I'll GIVE you some when I think you need it." That didn't set too well with me.

If I had it to do over again, I wouldn't have married so many times. Each ending was stressful; each divorce made me feel I had failed. A split set me back somewhat, although I recovered with a fresh spirit about three months later, but only after I met a new suitor.

Being alone bothered me. I didn't grieve too long after my divorces, but with Paul and Jim, I did. Both of them took me a lot longer to get over. As for my divorced husbands, I should have waited longer and gotten to know them. In the case of Raghbir, I should have had a prenuptial agreement. All of my quick decisions have seemed to stem from my OCD. I can understand that now as I look back over the years.

I haven't said much about Todd. As a mother, I think I failed, but I didn't know anything better to do. I wanted a father for him. That was my first thought in meeting a man. At the same time, I wanted Todd to be independent of me, but I allowed too much leeway to my parents. They were good for him in his early years, but, later, they tried to run his life the same way they did mine. Unfortunately, he attended a college about 45 miles away from them, and went to their house often, which he considered "home." They didn't like his friends or his way of life, and when I went to visit them, they would tell me all the "bad" things he was doing. I didn't know what to do and told my mother I didn't want to hear of it. She said, "You'd better listen and do something about him."

The best thing I could do was move to Delaware, where he joined me later. We didn't have any problems getting along. I let him live his life, and he let me live mine. He finished his degree at the University of Delaware and later moved to New Orleans, Louisiana. He and Paul got along very well and sometimes when he called, he didn't want to talk to me, but to Paul. He'd ask him about "girl stuff." He was on his way to see us in November of 1987 when he was killed in an auto accident. I grieved a long time over him, worrying about all the things I'd done wrong and how I could have done differently. This was during the time I was seeing Dr. Steg, and he helped very much.

CHAPTER 83

MY ADVICE to people with OCD is to get help early. You'll know when you have it to the extreme. I think most of us have it a little bit, we harbor superstitions or cling to the habitual way we do things. But when it bothers you, or a thought stays in your mind and eats at you, it's time to seek help. We know a lot more about psychology than we did nearly 70 years ago when I first went to a psychologist, and we are much more sympathetic than we once were. When I was young, we wanted to sweep the challenges of mental illness under the carpet and deny there was any disease in the family. Don't think you will outgrow it because you won't.

I've lived in an attractive, comfortable retirement home in Wilmington for almost four years. I'm in Independent Living, but they have Assisted Living, and the Starlight girls will come and help you if you need light work. They furnish a complimentary breakfast, and lunch or dinner every day. I go to dinner usually four times a week and save the extra credits to invite my friends for lunch or dinner. I have seven stepchildren and only a niece and nephew in

Missouri. Vicki and Jen are the children of Billie. She died two weeks after Jim and I were married in 2006. I miss her a lot.

Of all my accomplishments, I think getting my mental illness under control is the most important one. I have a nice apartment, a number of friends, and I keep busy. I don't drive anymore; I depend on the transportation provided here. I make greeting cards as a hobby and small business, but I've neglected them lately because I've been busy writing.

I'm an activist concerning the Black/White problem, probably because my hometown didn't allow African-Americans the privileges White people have, and I've always been interested in them. I would like to see non-violent probationers taught in prison to mentor young people in the neighborhood from which they came, giving them a livable salary so they won't turn to crime and drugs. As it stands, they will, of course, be sent back to prison, increasing the recidivism problem now facing our government leaders. Perhaps someday Afro-Americans can find their place in this country of all nationalities we call home.

And maybe someday obsessive-compulsive disorder treatment will be improved and better understood. That is my wish. I had a mild case, but it robbed me of my self-confidence, my thinking, my role as a daughter, wife, and mother, and of my childhood. I wouldn't wish the joy of childhood to be missed by anyone.

My final word to you is that if you are suffering, and need help, seek it before you have to give up the joys in your life. Know, there is hope for you to feel better and live better.

GALLERY

*Ned (Todd in the book) and me in Clay Center, KS. I was news editor of a
daily, the Clay Center Dispatch, and the only woman as an AP affiliate in the
state of Kansas at the time.
Ned was a senior in high school.*

Paul and me in my apartment after our marriage. We spent a short weekend at the St. Moritz Hotel in New York City, then later went on a honeymoon to Europe. This included Amsterdam, Paris and London. We missed the first night in Amsterdam because we had forgotten our passports. We went home after them, drank some champagne and didn't tell anyone. Our luggage was waiting for us in our hotel room when we got to Amsterdam the next day.

This is me on our trip to Italy. We had been to Spain the year before. I think we went to Finland in 1971.

354

I had my hair cut but not dyed. I was the same strawberry-blonde I had always been. The photo is just dark. We found the Greek people to be very friendly, and though it had been outlawed, we found that throwing cheap dishes was fun. Very cathartic, too.

Me at home. I like everything neat and clean but haven't cleaned since 1965—I hire it done. I hate cleaning the house but still spend a lot of time straightening. That's one reason I like it here. A cleaning lady comes in once a week to do the apartment.

Paul and me in Las Vegas. His oldest son, Jerry, was a photographer and took the picture. Jerry died in 2002 and one of Paul's other sons, Don, was killed by a motorcycle in 2005. When we were first married, Paul had four boys and one daughter, Marilyn, who now lives in Portland, OR. Ned was killed in a car crash in 1987 and I now have seven step-children, six boys and Marilyn. Jim Watson had four boys, two of whom are married.

Wilma, left, and me at Christmas in Missouri. I was living in Delaware at the time. Paul was Jewish and griped every Christmas about the many gifts I bought (on sale) during the year. I finally told him to let me enjoy my holiday the same as he enjoyed his. That put a stop to it. He often said that Christmas didn't mean much to him. Then, one year he complained to me that "I don't think your family gave me enough this year." (Yeah, from one who doesn't care much about Christmas. I had to laugh.)

Wilma (Billie in the book), right, and me on the fender of our father's car. I don't remember the dog's name or much about him. I only had two dogs in my lifetime: Wimpy, a Terrier mix, when Wilma and I were in elementary school, and Tuck, a Brittney Spaniel, when Ned was in his teens in Branson. We enjoyed both dogs.

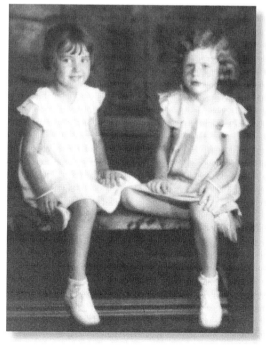

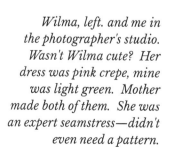

Wilma, left. and me in the photographer's studio. Wasn't Wilma cute? Her dress was pink crepe, mine was light green. Mother made both of them. She was an expert seamstress—didn't even need a pattern.

357

Jackie 1960

Jackie 18 months

*Jackie and her niece
Vicki Nelson 3-18-18*

ABOUT THE AUTHOR

JACQUELINE (Jackie) Gellens Watson grew up in a small town of 6,000 people in Southwest Missouri and firmly believes in small towns for children. "Everyone wants to know what you're doing, who you're going with, what trouble you've had lately, and any detail they can pass on as gossip. Single people should live in a city but, for children and married couples, you can't beat a small town."

She loves the small town she calls "home," but her work as a news editor and reporter took her elsewhere. The last place she worked was the twice-daily (now just once-daily) *News-Journal* newspaper in Wilmington, DE, where she lives now. She has resided in a nice retirement home with interesting people for nearly four years.

A graduate of Monett (MO) Junior College with an associate degree in English, Watson added to her education by attending night and weekend classes at Drury College in Springfield, MO; Kansas State College in Manhattan, KS; Southern Illinois University in Edwardsville, IL, and the University of Delaware in Wilmington during her newspaper career. She was mainly interested in writing and psychology courses and received her bachelor's degree in criminal justice and psychology from Wilmington College, now Wilmington University.

Watson spent the last eight years of her working experience as a mediator for Delaware Family Court and took early retirement at age 60 so she could accompany her husband, Paul Gellens, on their many travels.

She hopes you enjoy her book, and that it will help victims of obsessive-compulsive disorder. Watson says, "Everyone has a bit of it, some to the extreme when it becomes an illness. But with the proper doctoring and correct medication, it can be overcome. I still have a touch of it but know how to handle it—thanks to my many doctors and the right medications."

Watson makes greeting cards as a hobby and for her small business. She recently observed her 90th birthday at her home.

JACQUELINE GELLENS WATSON

Made in the USA
Middletown, DE
14 November 2019